OCEAN ADVENTURE

1840

GILLIAN NOAKES

Copyright © 2014 Gillian Noakes
All rights reserved.
ISBN-13: 978-1505767766

DEDICATION

The late Professor James McConville
whose valued tutorials gave direction to my research

ACKNOWLEDGEMENTS

Thanks are due to:

My Editor Philip Davies for his sound advice

My friend Daphne Statham for encouraging me to go on writing this book

Mr Giles de la Mare for reading the Final Draft, and giving me his opinion and advice

My sister Elizabeth Hunt for her help with the Title

My cousin, Patrick Wales-Smith for information about the Wales family and for his help with nautical details

My friend Jonathan King for helping me to publish the book as an e-book and for creating a cover

My cousin Rosemary Jackson Hunter for making the e-book a physical book

OCEAN ADVENTURE 1840

By Gillian Noakes

First Meeting

On a fine summer's day in 1840, Captain Douglas Wales, late of the Honourable East India Company and Master of the barque Orient, welcomed aboard his ship Madame Suzanne Volpélière, née Bérichon, and her daughter Barbe Amélie Laure Volpélière as passengers to Mauritius. Orient left London on August 2nd 1840 for Plymouth from where she continued on her journey on August 11th 1840. She was putting in at the island of Mauritius to take on fresh supplies of water and provisions for the passengers as well as a cargo of sugar. On board there were some 250 men, women and children, assisted passage emigrants, en route for Australia, who had started the voyage in London or

Plymouth, and eight passengers, including the Volpélières, who had paid for their passage.

Captain Wales had met Madame Volpélière and her daughter at mutual friends in London, where they had arrived from France on the first part of their journey to Mauritius, birthplace of them both, and where they were intending to reside permanently. Suzanne Volpélière still had relations amongst the French settlers who had fled to the tropical island from the French Revolutions in the eighteenth and nineteenth centuries. These aristocratic people had made their homes there, and had acquired land and property. Suzanne had married Henri Volpélière in Mauritius, where he also was born. Their marriage took place in 1821. Their daughter was born in Mauritius in 1822.

The couple later returned to Paris where Henri's sister Julie was becoming well known as a portrait painter and had useful contacts, and Henri became a lawyer at the court of the French king. His young daughter, known as Laure, was educated there and then studied piano at the Paris Conservatoire where it was said by her professors that she could have a brilliant future as a concert pianist, except that this was not thought a fit occupation for a young woman to pursue. But Suzanne had recently suffered a bitter blow in France when her husband Henri left her for a certain Madame Le Doux and there had been a separation. This led to her wish to return to her birthplace where there were sympathetic relations who would help her in her single, somewhat straitened circumstances.

Laure was, at eighteen, a very pretty young woman with dark eyes and hair. When she smiled, a dimple appeared in each cheek, giving her face an enchanting, mischievous look. Captain Wales had been attracted to her at first sight, and he was very happy that he would have the opportunity of continuing to see her on board his ship on the long journey ahead of them. He smiled at her now. She had been darting quick glances up at him and then looking modestly downwards, but she happily returned his smile having seen his on an upward glance. However, at a look of disapproval from her mother, she looked at the deck again.

The two women were beautifully clad in the fashion of the day, travelling dresses purchased in Paris made of fine, light wool. Laure's was a deep blue. Its sleeves were long and puffed from the elbow to the wrist; there was a cross-over bodice, made to be worn off the shoulder at evening time but filled in that day with three strips of material that matched the dress, and finished off with a lace fichu attached by a cameo brooch. The bodice was pointed down to a very small waist, and the outfit continued on to a full floor-length skirt that was bell shaped and kept thus by the addition of several stiff petticoats worn under it. Her bonnet was wide brimmed, matching the blue of her dress on the outside and lined inside with pale pink ruched satin to which was attached a cluster of white silk roses. Long, deeper pink silk ribbons were knotted together to keep the bonnet in place. If indoors, the ribbons would be left hanging on either side. The whole effect was to enhance her charming face. She wore a lavender coloured cashmere floor length shawl.

Suzanne wore a small indoor cap under her bonnet which was the fashion then for married women. Her bonnet was similar in size and shape, and russet coloured, but less decorated than her daughter's. Her dress had a beige background on which were vertical stripes on bodice and skirt that matched the colour of her bonnet. It had a large collar of the same material as the dress, and a separate, matching pelerine. Suzanne's shawl was brown.

The pair had brought with them from Paris Laure's Pleyel grand piano, which had been dismantled, each part wrapped in thick calico and then sacking, and was at present stored in one part of the hold of the ship with the rest of their luggage that was not needed on the journey. Amongst these items was the portrait of Laure that her aunt, Julie Volpélière, had painted when Laure was eleven years old. (Julie had made a name for herself as a portrait painter. Her tutor had been Serangeli, a pupil of Davide, famous for his monumental paintings of battles.)

Orient was bound for Port Phillip in Australia. She was carrying 15 barrels of pork, 7 barrels of flour, 7 cases of champagne, 7 cases of Hock, 151 battens, 151 water butts and 4 casks of oatmeal and pease. Also carried were 1 Durham cow, 1 bull calf, 1 Durham bull, 36 coils of cordage, 5 cases of cloth and cotton goods, the latter on order. There were also geese, ducks, chickens, pigs and sheep. Two paying passengers would join the ship at Mauritius.

OCEAN ADVENTURE 1840

Suzanne and Laure inspect their cabin

Suzanne and Laure were pleased with the accommodation they were to share on the journey. It was situated in the bows of the ship. One cabin had a patterned carpet and comfortable looking bunk beds, one above the other, whose sides could be pulled up for safety when the ship rolled and pitched. There was a metal wash hand-stand, bolted to the wall, the basin inserted into the top of the stand, a metal water jug beside it. Their clothes could be hung in a cupboard which was also bolted to the wall. For their comfort, there was a water closet to be flushed with seawater. Leading off the sleeping quarters was a tiny sitting room with two armchairs and a table.

"Very cosy," said Suzanne to Laure, once they had entered, "if somewhat cramped!"

"Look *Maman*! Someone has put a vase of flowers on the table," exclaimed Laure. "Do you think it could have been Captain Wales' idea?"

"I doubt it my child; he is a bluff, seafaring man," Suzanne replied.

On the ship there were a number of stewards to tend to the paying passengers' needs, to deal with the cabin passengers' and the crew's washing (this was an extremely important task as it helped to keep illness at bay) and cooks in the main galley for the crew and passengers. The crew was comprised of sailors of a variety of nationalities Their accommodation was below that of the cabin passengers consisting of hammocks slung in the fo'c'sle of the ship.

The mother and daughter conversed in French. Suzanne knew no English and Laure only a very little from her schooling in Paris. Their friends in London had acted as interpreters for the pair when they were making their arrangements to sail with Captain Wales.

It was obvious to Suzanne that her daughter had been immediately taken with Douglas Wales. Laure had led a sheltered life in Paris spending many hours at the piano each day, and taking healthy walks for exercise in the Champs-Elysées with her mother. She and her mother called on friends and sometimes she played at the musical soirées they would arrange. There had so far been no serious suitor although one or two young men had shown their admiration of her looks and her talent. Notes had been written and received. Male fellow students at the Conservatoire carried her music and sent posies of flowers. Laure knew that she was beautiful and attractive to the opposite sex, but she was not a flirt.

Douglas Wales was nothing like the young men in Paris! To begin with he was fourteen years her senior, thirty-two to her eighteen. His religion was Anglican, hers Roman Catholic. They hardly spoke each other's language. He was, however, tall and handsome with dark brown hair and hazel coloured eyes. If his nose was a trifle long, it was straight and he had a sensitive mouth with a full lower lip. Because of his seaboard life, his complexion was ruddy. He was an excellent Master of his ship, liked by his crew, which included 1st Mate G.D.

Pritt, 2nd Mate A. Brooking and 3rd Mate William Maurice. Also on board was Surgeon Superintendent Grant.

As the mother and daughter began to unpack and put their clothes away, they heard the rattling of the raising of the anchor, and felt the ship vibrate as, towed from the harbour by a steam tug, she slowly moved out towards the open sea. There was the thump of the sailors' feet as they ran about the wooden deck above, casting off the mooring lines at the stern and preparing to raise the sails on her three masts and then securing the heavy anchor ropes to the capstan. Some hands climbed aloft the masts to unfurl the sails.

The ship

Orient was a three masted barque of 596 tons. According to her Lloyd's rating of 1838 she was particularly suitable for use as an emigrant vessel and for carrying perishable goods anywhere in the world. The weather was fair.

"God speed our ship!" said Douglas from the quarterdeck. He always remembered to entrust his ship and all who sailed in her to the Almighty. For all her size, 124ft in length and 25ft in width, Orient seemed to her Master to breast the waves lightly.

When the ship was well under way Suzanne and Laure passed through a door in their sitting room to the saloon where they would join Douglas and other cabin passengers for the evening meal. There were two young couples, and two single gentlemen, one of whom was a clergyman on his way to take up his calling in Mauritius.

The other was a schoolmaster who would spend the voyage giving lessons to the emigrant children and any adults who so desired.

The ladies had removed the panels of material from the bodices of their dresses, and so were bare shouldered. Douglas admired Laure's décolletage, but did not let his gaze linger too long on it. He had realized that Suzanne Volpélière was disapproving of the possibility of any romantic ideas occurring on either his or Laure's side!

Douglas' observations about Madame Volpélière

Suzanne had made it clear that she was an aristocratic person, whereas Douglas certainly was not. Why, he couldn't even hold a conversation of any great length with her in French! Privately, Douglas was slightly amused by her attitude. The French escapées from the guillotine who had settled in Mauritius, and had been so loathe to give up their Madagascarene slaves, were not the sort of people he respected. He much preferred the down to earth English couples who were bravely setting off for a life in Australia. They were interested in everything he could tell them about shipboard matters, affairs of trade, and anything he knew about the colonies.

The conversation flowed easily, all in English of course, Douglas trying from time to time to exercise his few words of French in order that his two French passengers did not feel completely left out. Laure thought to herself that he was extremely kind to do this, and she tried to help him out when he struggled to express himself.

Henry Manning, the clergyman, did speak French fluently, and he made every effort to engage Laure in conversation. When he found out that she was a pianist, he felt they had a great deal in common as he played the flute and had a moderately fine singing voice.

"We have entertainments on board for all the passengers," said Douglas to Henry, "some dancing and singing. Perhaps you would consent to play some jigs?" The clergyman looked startled, "A jig?" he asked. "Yes," said Douglas, "something they can dance to – something catchy." "Well..." Henry replied, "I think I might have something amongst my music that I could adapt. I'll have a look." Laure in the meantime had hardly managed to stifle her amusement when Henry interpreted this interchange for her in French. She and the clergyman had been discussing classical composers for pianoforte and other instruments, and Henry was obviously a knowledgeable and serious classical musician, as was she. A jig sounded so out of place. Her face had become quite flushed, so much so that her mother made a disapproving clucking sound and said, "Laure, finish up your dessert; we need to go early to our beds. We have had a very tiring day."

"Will you not take some coffee?" said Douglas, as mother and daughter started to rise from the table, reluctant to see Laure leave. Suzanne agreed to stay, and the meal continued pleasantly.

In those days at sea the male passengers, some of the assisted emigrants included, were allowed to remain on deck until midnight, but all the females had to go below at 8 pm. Laure felt this to be very unfair. She would have enjoyed being on deck, benefitting from the sea breeze and watching the phosphorescent light on the tops of the waves. It was stuffy and not well ventilated in their cabins. A steward had put hot salt water in the jug for washing; there was saltwater soap, and Suzanne was already making her toilet preparatory to going to her bed in the lower bunk.

"I shall just sit up a little, *Maman*," said Laure, "and read."

"Make sure to read something from the Bible," said Suzanne; "leave your novel until tomorrow."

Laure sighed, but acquiesced, leaving her novel on the table and taking up her Bible. However, she did not read at all, but sat thinking. She missed her father. He was more light-hearted than her mother, and would sometimes encourage her to rebel. "Don't practise any longer, *ma chére*," he would say. "Come out in the carriage. Your mother is resting, she will only know about our escapade after it has happened – not before!" He often felt constrained during his marriage to Suzanne to behave in a way that was contrary to his somewhat ebullient nature. Laure understood that the contrast Madame Le Doux presented had been too great a temptation for Henri to resist. Suzanne was reserved and religious and of a serious disposition, whereas Madame Le Doux was a very vivacious lady who loved parties and society gossip. She took part in the theatricals that were popular in private houses and was indeed a merry widow with a roving eye. Henri had been flattered that she fell in love with him. She had made this quite clear at the outset. It had not been difficult for him to leave Suzanne, and they had obtained a judicial separation. (Divorce in France was not accepted until 1848.)

Douglas Wales in the meantime also had much to think about that evening. Amongst the steerage passengers from England were some twenty young females who had succeeded in obtaining false references that would enable them to emigrate from various unscrupulous clergymen in exchange for cash. These men of the cloth waited at ports for this express purpose. The practice continued until it was declared illegal when the screening of prospective passengers became much stricter.

Mr Pritt, first mate, had reported to Douglas that afternoon that these twenty young women were behaving in a very indecorous way on deck and that the sailors were becoming distracted from their work because of these flirtatious females. Some of the married couples who were taking the air on deck were also caused consternation since the wives thought their husbands were showing too much interest in these hussies. Mr Pritt added that these girls were "no better than they ought to be", and hinted to Douglas that he felt sure some of them had been following the oldest profession back in England.

Douglas had dealt with many problems inherent in sailing an emigrant vessel around the world, but this particular situation was the first of its kind that he had encountered. He needed to take swift action, and so ordered all the young women below deck immediately, putting them under the care of a matron and three constables who were appointed by their overall chief, Surgeon Superintendent Grant, to keep order amongst the emigrants. The girls were set immediately to work at whatever task could be suitable for them. This was mainly as laundry maids, emptying chamber pots, cleaning the "'tween deck", or peeling vegetables in the galley kitchen. The girls were none too pleased. They found to their further discontent that they were to be in bed by 10 pm in the stern section of the steerage deck allocated to single women. Single men were situated a long way off in the bows of the ship! Married couples' quarters separated the two sexes.

When the voyage was into its second week Douglas went to the quarterdeck to begin his watch at 8 pm and his thoughts turned to the attractive French girl, Laure, and her mother. His watch would not end until midnight. On some ships the master never did a watch at all, leaving all that to the first mate and two helmsmen on the wheel. Douglas however was a fair man who wanted all who sailed in his ship to know that he was an active participant in the whole running of it. The sailors respected him. He was also a good disciplinarian, witness the way he had dealt swiftly with the unruly girls.

Douglas decides to act

Because Douglas wished to spend some time with Laure, he decided to ask her mother if she and her daughter would walk on the poop deck with him the next day, weather permitting. Passengers were able to exercise on deck by walking up and down it – somewhat like sentries.

Douglas, having observed that Suzanne Volpélière was not greatly in favour of his interest in her daughter, and even less so of the interest he had begun to believe Laure to have for him, knew that he would have to prove himself to be a worthy suitor for Laure's hand in marriage. It was time he married. He was thirty-two. Laure was not the first young woman he had been attracted to, but coming from a devout Christian background he had not been one to have a girl in every port! He however knew enough about young females to enable him to interpret the signals, and Laure's glances had told of her liking for him. He must find ways to change Suzanne's feelings about his courtship of her daughter. "What reason can this mother have to be against the possibility of her daughter making a good match?" Douglas thought. "I may be considerably older than her daughter, but my ship is my own, I am a man of substance. It must be one of religion."

"Laure has such a dear little face," he thought, "and her hands are so beautiful. I would very much like to hear her play the piano." He thought about her piano in the hold, and decided to go down himself to the hold and check that it was securely fastened and not in danger of being thrown about in bad weather. Henry Manning had told Douglas that, from his conversations with Laure, he had learned of her studies at the Paris Conservatoire of Music.

The walk on deck

The next day was a fine one, and at breakfast Douglas, having asked Henry to assist with translation, broached the subject of the promenade on the poop deck to Suzanne and Laure. Laure immediately stated that she thought this was a most excellent idea.

"*Maman*, it would be so nice to take the air and look at the sky again, and it is good weather today. Please let us go with the captain."

Suzanne turned to Henry and said in French, "But do we need the captain to escort us? Can passengers not exercise on deck without taking him from his post? Surely he has many more important tasks to complete?"

"Indeed *Madame*," replied Douglas courteously, after hearing the translation, "passengers may do so, but it would give me great pleasure to practise what little French I have in conversation with you and your daughter."

On hearing Henry's translation and finding the captain's humility much to her liking, Suzanne acquiesced, and it was decided that the promenade would start at 11 o'clock. Douglas had asked Henry Manning to join them. He and Laure walked behind Douglas and Suzanne, Douglas turning from time to time to address Laure, pointing out to her various objects on the deck and their uses (Henry translating when Laure's English deserted her).

When Laure realized that the promenade would only consist of walking up and down the poop deck, and when she saw that there was great activity going on below on the middle deck with all sorts of people engaged in many different tasks, she asked if they could go down there too. Suzanne was horrified at the idea of doing this. "It would not be seemly to mingle with those who are travelling in the emigrant quarters, nor the sailors on that deck!" she said. "Look, there are animals there too and there is washing hung out to dry!"

Laure laughed. "It is like Noah's Ark," she said. There were sheep and pigs in pens on the deck and above them hens, ducks and geese in coops which had been placed in a boat. A cow looked over the door of a shed. Women were washing clothes in tubs and buckets filled with rainwater previously collected, and hanging the wet clothes out on the rigging. A sailor was playing an accordion.

"I will protect your daughter, *Madame*," Douglas told Suzanne, "and Mr Manning and the married couples will be with us too." Suzanne eventually capitulated, and deciding to stay where she was she watched her daughter, the captain, Henry Manning and the rest of the group descend a ladder to the middle deck.

Laure was now walking with Douglas, who offered her his arm. "Captain Wales," she said in English (Douglas being entranced to hear his name spoken with a French accent), "what are those people doing?" She was looking at men and women standing in front of pots that were hung on a bar above a long iron brazier. It was immediately in front of a building which had a sliding door that was slightly open. It was facing the middle mast.

"The steerage passengers cook their rations there, *Mademoiselle*," answered Douglas.

"And the building near to them, what is that?" Laure asked when Henry had made the necessary translation. She could see freshly killed poultry hanging inside and outside it.

Douglas said, in English, that it was where the ship's butchers slaughtered fowl and animals for the cabin passengers' table. (Henry Manning deftly translated throughout the conversation.) Douglas told Laure that the brazier was extremely popular because cooking could take place in the open air.

Each steerage passenger received every week preserved meat, 5lbs of oatmeal, 2½lbs of biscuit, 1lb four, 2lbs rice, ½lb sugar and 2 ounces of tea as well as coffee, and in Orient there was a main galley where food for everyone, officers and crew and all category of passengers was prepared.

Douglas was well aware how uncomfortable the accommodation could be for emigrant passengers who had bunks in the 'tween deck, or steerage part of the ship, between the cabins for paying passengers and the hold. He abided by the new laws that had been made in Europe regarding conditions for the steerage passengers, but even so shipboard life for an emigrant in the 'tween deck could never be ideal. In bad weather the hatches had to be battened down and the few portholes closed, leading to a lack of ventilation that was very unpleasant due to seasickness amongst them. Some of the emigrants were quite unable to leave their bunks at all because of seasickness. Sanitation, consisting of chamber pots and buckets behind rudimentary sacking curtains, which could fall over and empty their contents when the ship pitched or rolled, would add to the stench. It would not be possible for men to use the water closets situated on the sheltered side of the ship's main deck as it would be unsafe to do so in stormy weather. Women and children would find it impossible to leave their bunks and get to the enclosed water closet facilities.

Had the hatches not been closed though, the ship's taking in water would have caused flooding of the 'tween deck, leading to much discomfort and the potential for illness amongst the emigrants. Douglas insisted that the able-bodied male emigrants scraped the deck to keep down disease. This was done every day on a roster.

For fairness, groups of passengers were selected to allocate provisions each day for their fellow emigrants and certain steerage passengers were chosen to take responsibility for the conduct and health of them all.

"We are so lucky, *Maman*," Laure had said that morning, "that we had enough money to pay for our cabins. I do hope the emigrants will find a much better life for themselves and their families at the end of this journey."

Suzanne had smiled wryly. "We had only just enough money, my child," she said, thinking about her errant husband's unkind treatment of his wife and daughter regarding financial matters. Other than their clothes and a few items of jewellery, and the grand piano, Suzanne and Laure had very little money left over after the cost of their passage to Mauritius. This was the reason that Suzanne had decided to rejoin members of her family who still lived in Mauritius. Her sister had written that she would be glad to be of assistance to Suzanne and Laure if they returned there. Suzanne hoped that a suitable husband would be found for Laure amongst the French inhabitants of Mauritius.

In the queue in front of the brazier, Laure noticed a young woman with a small child holding onto her skirt. The girl was about the same age as Laure, who wondered what it would be like to have a little child to care for, and what it felt like when the child was in the womb. She had heard the servants in the Paris house speaking in low tones about such matters, but her mother, when asked what marriage and childbirth was like, had replied, "You will find out later!" Laure hoped that she would do so one day, and that a kind and gentle husband would be her instructor. She smiled at the woman, who returned her smile.

"What are you going to cook?" Laure asked in English. "I have coffee and porridge oats," replied the girl. "We have been supplied with food, quite a lot more than we ever had in England. I have some raisins, too, to put on the porridge, which will please my little boy."

"What is his name?" Laure asked. "Georgy – Georgy Henry, after his father." "Is his father on the ship too?" Laure enquired.

"Oh yes, Miss; we wouldn't have been allowed to embark without him. He is at work with others, cleaning the deck in our quarters. The Captain has ordered that this is to be done every morning. George also has the task of pumping the bilges with others."

The young woman went on to explain that, according the rules of the commissioners, to be allowed to emigrate candidates had to be sober, industrious and of general good moral character and also should have such skills as were the most needed in the colony. They were required to produce certificates to this effect. They must also be in good health, and all the adults needed to be capable of labour and going out to work for wages. The authorities found young married couples without children the most acceptable candidates. No single women with children and no widows with children would be allowed to emigrate. Anyone falsifying any part of the application form for an assisted passage to a colony could be fined up to £50 – a huge sum in those days.

The Storm

The weather had been fine that morning, and everybody on deck had enjoyed the warm sunshine and sea breezes, but Douglas had noticed that the wind was picking up and that there was a patch of dark cloud to the west of the ship, so he decided to bring the outing for the passengers to a close. From his long experience as an ocean voyager, he immediately gave the order for sail to be reduced to ready the ship for the coming storm. In this way he made sure that as far as possible he was securing the safety of his precious human cargo and his crew. He went up to the quarterdeck. Already the two helmsmen needed to work harder because of the wind which was increasing in strength every minute. It grew stronger and the sea, from being calm and shimmering in the sun, with shoals of dolphin happily jumping and diving into it as they followed the ship, became agitated. It formed itself into waves which struck the upper parts of the ship in endless succession as she forged forwards. The sky darkened and soon afterwards rain began to fall, a light rain at first, but gradually increasing in volume until it pelted down onto the decks. As though to respond to this downpour, the wind whipped the waves up until they grew in size causing the ship to rise up with a wave, only to tip down and crash forward into the trough beyond before the next wave reared up to its full height and this action was repeated. A sudden crack of thunder preceded a dazzling flash of lightning. The crew were hard at work, following Douglas' orders, but the violent motion of the ship made moving about its decks very hazardous for them.

In the emigrants' part of the ship most people were very frightened and calling out, "Lord, have mercy! We are all going down with the ship! We will all be lost." A large number of them began to suffer from seasickness, which added to their misery.

People held on to the sides of their bunks to prevent themselves falling out when the ship pitched and rolled about in the storm, but water kegs, cans, teapots, buckets and innumerable other things were thrown off the shelves and added to the noise of the wind, thunder and rain by being hurled from one side of the deck to the other, making a horrible clanging sound because most of them were made of tin. Little Georgy and his mother, Jane, were both afraid.

Jane tried to comfort her child by crooning some nursery rhymes to him. She held him close in her arms and rocked him. Her husband George was stretched out full-length beside them. He was exhausted after the day's work. Certain male emigrants, of whom George was one, were expected, as well as cleaning the deck each morning, to help the sailors with the management of the sails. George had done his best to help the crew to hoist the sails, but had received many curses owing to his clumsiness in making the knots, and the fact that he was not nimble enough on his feet to be in the right place at the right time. He also had to help pump the bilges and fill the water tanks, and that morning he had carried his family's bedding up on deck so that it might be aired in the sun. The Captain insisted on this in a further attempt to keep disease at bay.

George was worried that the fierce wind might lift the tarpaulins that had been lashed over the gratings on the deck and let water down into the steerage accommodation soaking the bedding as waves washed over the ship. These tarpaulins had been lashed to the raised borders of the hatches, and caused the worsening of the lack of light and air in the emigrants' quarters.

Because of the storm it was not possible for the groups of emigrants responsible for collecting and cooking the provisions to provide the midday meal. Moving about was impossible. All they could do was stay holding fast in their bunks and those who were not seasick hoped that the pangs of hunger would abate. Jane and George had kept their freshwater ration safe in a can with a lid and handle. This Jane had propped upright behind her against the wooden wall.

Each emigrant was given three quarts of fresh water per day, but most of them preferred the taste of the rainwater which, when it came, they would collect in whatever utensil came to hand.

To add to the misery of being in a rolling pitching ship, the four large oil lamps in the 'tween deck had to be extinguished in case their falling from their hooks on the ceiling resulted in the setting of fires. So it was pitch dark, which made the emigrant passengers feel disorientated. Most held onto their neighbours in the bunks, husbands to wives, children to mothers, brothers and sisters to each other. Babies wailed. There was a solitary episode of light relief when a barrel of beer fell from the bunk of one of the male emigrants and he joined it, clasping his arms around it only to be thrown from one side of the 'tween deck to the other, still holding on to it. The few other steerage passengers who were not feeling too seasick raised a laugh and the owner of the barrel cursed them as he rolled past.

Meanwhile in their sleeping cabin, Suzanne and Laure endeavoured to keep calm and be as comfortable as possible. Although both had made sea voyages before, this storm was the fiercest that either of them had experienced. Suzanne soon began to suffer from seasickness, although Laure found that she was not so afflicted. Suzanne lay prostrate in the lower bunk. Laure pulled the sides up for safety's sake, and covered her mother with a blanket. She gave Suzanne sips of water and held the basin when her mother vomited. She then emptied the basin down the lavatory in their cabin. This was really quite rudimentary as everything fell down into the sea, and it was supplied with a leather flap to prevent the users' nether regions being splashed.

"You must keep drinking, *Maman*," Laure said, "even if it makes you sick. Otherwise you will suffer much more." Suzanne groaned and shut her eyes. Eventually, she seemed to doze off, and Laure climbed the ladder up to her top bunk. There she lay listening to the storm and thinking about Douglas Wales. What was he doing now? Was he on the quarterdeck with his crew? Was he in danger? She had seen as they walked on deck how the sailors showed their respect for him, saluting him as he passed them, if they had a hand free to do so. "He has a very pleasant smile," thought Laure, "and he was extremely patient with me when I tried to speak to him in English. I shall have to try to improve in that language." Laure decided to ask John Browning, the ship's schoolmaster, if she could borrow an English book. "I think quite a simple reading book, suitable for a child," she thought. "It is best always to begin studying something simple before one goes on to something more difficult."

Suzanne was continuously unwell and unable to leave her bunk, so Laure was kept busy with nursing duties. Meals were provided for the paying passengers in the saloon, but not all of them came to take advantage of them.

That evening Laure made her way through to the saloon having assured herself that Suzanne was comfortable. Laure felt quite hungry as she had not been able to attend for the midday meal due to her mother's distress. Douglas and the two single men were the only people at the table, enjoying the first course of the dinner, which was roast pork, roast potatoes and green vegetables. A pig had been killed that morning so that the paying passengers could be served fresh meat.

"Do the assisted emigrants have fresh meat Captain Wales?" asked Laure hesitantly in English.

"I'm afraid not. There wouldn't be room for enough animals to supply all the steerage passengers," Douglas replied. "They are allocated preserved salted meat which makes quite an appetizing stew. Each emigrant's ration of meat is put in a muslin bag with their name on it, and the cook boils them all together in a large utensil. When it is cooked, vegetables can be added. Dried peas and lentils make it a sustaining meal."

Laure turned to Henry Manning for an accurate translation of several of the words spoken by Douglas.

"It is sad that there is such a difference between people's position in life, that those most in need of good food have to make do with mediocre provisions, whilst those who throughout their lives, have never known hunger are given the best of everything," she said in her own language.

"But, *Mademoiselle*," interjected Henry in French, "at home in England they are much worse off. In some cottages in the deep countryside, gruel is the only food the people can afford! There has recently been a disease of the crops which has caused famine in many parts of the land. Not long ago some weavers residing at Bolton in Lancashire presented a petition to the Colonial Secretary of State requesting that they and their families might be transported to any British settlement. They could no longer find employment due to competition with machines and they were not able to turn to any other form of trade. Sadly they were turned down for no British settlement had need of their craft."

Laure remembered what the young woman had told her at the brazier on deck that morning, and realized that not to nourish herself would not help those less fortunate than herself to obtain more fresh food. Her previous hours' fasting had left her with a good appetite and she continued to enjoy her meal.

Douglas was pleased that Laure had a good heart when Henry Manning told him what she had said. What Douglas had heard about the attitude to life of the French aristocracy in Mauritius and other parts of their Empire had led him to believe that they were deeply entrenched in the idea that they belonged to a superior class and because of this were entitled to the good things in life. He refrained from attempting a discussion in either French or English fearing that Laure might misunderstand and gain the impression that he disapproved of her too. There was also the fact that he himself had had many advantages in life in comparison to the emigrants who, he knew, must be experiencing a very unpleasant time in their quarters on the ship, which seemed then to be tossed about all directions by the fury of mountainous waves which crashed constantly over its decks.

Douglas, after he had finished his meal, made his excuses quickly to return to the quarterdeck. He had noticed that the violent motion of the ship in the storm was different and once on deck again it was immediately evident to him that the wind had changed and become stronger. He shouted a change of course to the two helmsmen to reduce the crashing of the ship through the big seas, while accepting that this new course would lengthen the voyage. It was very cold on deck even though Douglas and his officers were wrapped in their greatcoats, and Douglas was concerned about the emigrant passengers in the 'tween deck. He knew that they would be in the dark as well as being cold and fearful.

"If the storm has abated by morning, I shall get them all up in groups on deck for an hour or so of fresh air and exercise," Douglas thought. "Poor souls, little did some of them know what a sea journey would be like. Many had never seen the sea in their lives before. I hope we will not have too many deaths." At this stage in the journey there had been no sign of any disease that could cause an epidemic. The food was wholesome. Douglas had made sure that the suppliers of the preserved meat he had taken on board for the emigrants were honest and that the meat was of the best quality. There had been a recent case of a shipload of emigrants bound for New Zealand being supplied with inferior meat by unscrupulous merchants that was the cause of an epidemic of diarrhoea and vomiting, and many of the emigrants, especially children, had died.

The storm raged for the whole night, but by dawn the wind had dropped and when the sun was fully risen it warmed the ship's crew and gradually dried the sodden deck. Orient became comparatively easy to navigate, in contrast to the helmsmen's struggles on the wheel that night and those of the crew responsible for the sails. These were heavily waterlogged at first, but then, as with the deck, they started to dry out and to be ready for repair.

Douglas went to his cabin to change into dry clothes after washing and shaving. He then allowed himself a brief rest in an armchair before he returned to the deck to supervise the lifting of the hatches to alleviate the distress of the steerage passengers after such a fraught night. His first action was to order the quartermaster to burn sulphur and vinegar in the 'tween deck to reduce the dreadful odours that had resulted from so many people being closed in unventilated conditions for hours on end. Dr Grant, the surgeon on board, reported to Douglas that there were at least a dozen people with broken bones, cuts and bruises, and one man who had a cut head. Thankfully, he was able to report that there had been no deaths. Indeed there had been the birth of a baby and in spite of the conditions of her confinement, both mother and child had survived.

"Get oatmeal ready for all who can eat, and set the men to work cleaning the accommodation," was Douglas' next order. His officers went about carrying out his instructions, and Douglas went below to breakfast.

Douglas describes rescue of passengers from foundering ship

The only other person at breakfast when he reached the saloon was Laure. He smiled at her and said, this time in halting French, "You must be a good sailor, *Mademoiselle*. I presume none of the others are inclined to take breakfast."

"I think I saw a steward taking tea to one or two cabins," Laure replied. She continued, in a mixture of French and English: "I am surprised at having tolerated the storm so well. It was the shrieking of the wind in the sails that dismayed me most of all. It was such a seemingly unholy sound, like souls in Hell." Douglas nodded in agreement. He took bacon and eggs from the dish a steward held out to him.

"How is your mother now?" he asked. Laure told him that Suzanne was a little better, not being seasick any longer, but feeling very weak and tired.

"I will make sure that she is sent some beef tea as soon as she feels able to take it," promised Douglas.

John Browning, the schoolmaster, then came in, looking a little pale, but having made an effort to be as well groomed as possible.

"What a night!" he exclaimed and helped himself from the coffee pot on the table. Turning to Douglas he went on: "Captain, you must be used to this sort of weather. Were we in danger at any time?"

"Well", said Douglas, "if we had stayed in a position surrounded by such gigantic waves as there were at the worst of the storm, Orient might well have capsized and been dragged down by the soaking sails. That is why I took a different course and why it will be a little longer before we reach our destination."

"Thank God for that!" said Browning. Then Laure, who had understood Douglas this time, chiefly because of the import of his words which he had delivered in a slow, serious tone, said, "Captain Wales, do you have time to relate to us any adventure you have had on your voyages?"

Douglas looked at his pocket watch and said, "I have enough time, I believe." He continued: "During a voyage I made in 1839 on my way homeward to England, after delivering all my passengers to their destination, I sailed northwards along the Grand Barrier. I shall speak slowly and pause so that Mademoiselle Laure can let me know if she has not fully understood me. Then I shall try to translate into French. What a pity Mr Manning is not with us! I shall do my best."

"I have a little of the language, Captain," said John. "I can assist maybe."

John and Laure looked eagerly towards Douglas who then began what was to be a most exciting tale, made even more so because it was a true account.

"On 4th May 1839, Orient left Sydney in company with the ship Aliquie. The captain of the Aliquie had requested that we kept in company with him along the coast. We had heard, just as we were leaving Sydney, that three ships had been lost already that year on the numerous reefs of the Grand Barrier. This is a reef extending all the way from the eastern extreme of New Guinea to about 20 degrees south along the coast of New Holland." Douglas stopped to explain to Laure what 'reef' meant and that the Grand Barrier Reef was made up of many different varieties of underwater coral gardens and that the coral was very sharp and could cause great damage to ships. John Browning interpreted for Douglas.

"We had a fine run to the north and on the noon of May 13th were about 120 miles from the Grand Barrier," he continued. "There are many passages through these coral reefs but most of them are extremely narrow. We steered for a point that for the past few years has been passed through by many ships."

"You had records of this, Sir?" asked John.

"Yes, and somewhat rudimentary maps, but no one in Orient had been there before. At 6 am we saw from the masthead that there were high breakers as far as the eye could reach, north and south. They looked very unfriendly indeed! Orient was being steered right towards them, so, on getting within a mile of them, we skirted along their edge to find some opening. In the course of two hours we found that we had been drifted by a strong current considerably to the north of the opening we had intended to pass through and that to get back to it was impossible." Douglas paused and the schoolmaster was able to do some translating which left Laure with her heart in her mouth at the thought of the terrible danger the captain and all his crew had been in. She was glad that Douglas was present and telling the story himself.

"We then steered away north until we had high breakers in every direction around the ship," continued Douglas. "A passage had to be found somewhere, so we found and aimed for a clear looking spot, and were able to pass through a narrow gap between two dry sand banks. Ten minutes later we were in sixteen fathoms of smooth water! Here we thankfully let the sails out so that we stopped, or 'hove-to' as we sailors say, until noon when we ascertained our position. We found that we had been driven twenty five miles north of our proper position by currents.

"Well, we were in, that was one good thing, so we steered for a part of the strait better known and at 3 am anchored where we were sheltered from the direction of the wind by some sand hills, and reefs. The following day we again proceeded and manoeuvred our way through the numerous, or rather innumerable, reefs that cover this dangerous track. After an exceedingly anxious day, we again sailed up into the wind, stopped the ship and anchored for the night. The next morning we had by 10 o'clock reached the north extreme of New Holland, and I was congratulating my officers on the prospect of being clear of the strait in three or four hours, when we discovered a ship about twelve miles from us with signals of distress flying and firing guns.

From the masthead in the direction in which she lay, there was nothing to be seen but extensive reefs surrounded with breakers. I, however, tried to get Orient near her to render any assistance, but after making progress against the wind by tacking with a strong breeze for about three hours, I found that we were only losing ground. In consequence I headed into the direction of the wind and anchored under Albany Island, about sixteen miles from her. As I knew that Aliquie was astern and would soon catch us up, I determined to wait and consult with the captain as to what measure we should adopt."

"Those in the distressed vessel must have wondered whether you and your men were going to try to save them," said John. "Imagine, *Mademoiselle*!" And turning to Laure he related in French what Douglas had said. "*Mon Dieu*, yes!" she said when she realized the situation the captain and crew of Orient had found themselves in. Her admiration for the gallant captain, always present, increased greatly as she realized what a brave, kind man he was, prepared to endeavour a rescue attempt in such appalling conditions.

Douglas continued: "Aliquie soon arrived and, after talking the matter over with her captain, we agreed that we would each send a boat at daylight. Accordingly he sent his chief mate (because his wife would not allow **him** to go), and I went with seven men in our cutter."

Douglas then addressed John Browning and said, "Please tell Mademoiselle Laure that the term "cutter" means a boat that can be rowed as well as put to sail. It is carried by large ships for transporting passengers or crew members ashore, or for rescue purposes."

He continued: "We had a tedious, dangerous row – sixteen miles through coral reefs with a very high sea, but in six hours we reached her. She had broken her anchor two nights previously, and there was an extensive coral reef nearby with waves breaking in every direction. Her crew were in a state little short of mutiny and if our boats' crews had not been able to prevent this they would have run away with the boats and left the captain and passengers to shift for themselves. They even, while we were on board, formed a plan to break into the hold and steal the rum. They tried to persuade our men to join them in this plan. Our men came to me and told me of this, and in order to prevent anything of the sort we loaded our firearms and threw all the spirits overboard. This set of the greatest scoundrels the world had ever produced swore at us furiously, and my men and the other ship's men came to me and said that they would do anything to keep order. I had some trouble restraining them from setting to work and thrashing the villainous crew of the foundering ship, they were so indignant at their unmanly behaviour."

Douglas stopped again to let John Browning translate for Laure's benefit, and Laure took the opportunity to say to

John, "I should be grateful if you could let me have some books of English words and grammar so that I can become more familiar with Captain Wales' language and not need constant assistance in understanding it." John assured her that he would provide her with appropriate books and would help her if she wished. Douglas continued:

"We tried every way to get the ship off the reef without any effect, therefore having set fire to her and killed the horses and livestock we embarked the crew and passengers in the boats and brought them over to Orient. I brought the captain's wife with me – the poor thing did nothing but cry all the way – and the boat being very deep in the water, with all the luggage, was nearly swamped! I brought the captain, his wife, the passengers and half the ship's company, and the other boat took the remainder."

"How lucky those mutinying crewmen were to be treated with such compassion," said John. "Other rescuers might not have been inclined to fill up the boats with such scoundrels."

"How did you feel when you finally had everyone back on board Orient?" asked Laure in English, stumbling over some of the words.

"Well," said Douglas, "it had been a period of great excitement to me, passing those coral reefs, then assisting the foundering ship. We had been constantly exposed to the sun, and there had been no let up from anxiety, so when we got clear of the reef it took several days to bring my pulse down to its regular beat! But once we continued with a comparatively easy navigation I was again happy. Orient is a capital sea boat."

It was then that Laure started to question the nature of her feelings for Douglas. That she admired him, she already knew, but when the sound of his voice seemed to reach into her heart, causing a sharp intake of breath, she began to ask herself why this was. Why was she now giving his mouth such attention? Why was she noticing that his eyelashes were thick enough to make a woman envious, that his hair had a natural wave, and that a lock of it brushed his forehead? What was there about his long-fingered hands that held her gaze? Laure's emotions were new to her and she clasped her hands together and looked down at the table attempting to control them. It was not long however before she was unable to prevent herself from looking straight into Douglas' eyes and smiling at him. Douglas' heart beat more quickly as he understood from Laure's expression that her feelings for him were strengthening. He would have liked to take her face in his hands and kiss her on her cheeks and lips, to go down on bended knee and propose to her! All he could do at that moment was to say, "*Mademoiselle*, you have been a most receptive audience. I hope you have understood me and enjoyed my adventurous tale." To which Laure nodded her affirmation, speechless in any language because of the overwhelming rush of feeling she was experiencing.

It suddenly occurred to Laure how much she would like to take Douglas' hands in hers and tell him that she loved him. She became rosy with blushes at this thought, rose hastily to her feet, and said in English, "I must now go to my *Maman* to attend her, *excusez-mois, s'il-vous-plait.*" She almost ran from the saloon.

Suzanne considers her motives

Once back in their suite, Laure composed herself before approaching her mother.

Suzanne was sitting up in her bunk, writing. She was using a pencil rather than a pen, fearing that having an inkwell near her might lead to splashes of ink falling on her bed jacket or on the sheets. Suzanne was an avid letter writer. She wrote to her family in Mauritius, and when she lived in Paris to her friends in France, to members of her husband's family, and to her daughter's tutors at the Conservatoire. There had even been once, to Laure's dismay, a letter to the parents of a certain young man who had called on Laure bearing the gift of a piano piece he had composed and wished her to have and to play. Laure being only seventeen at the time, and the young man not much older – a fellow student – Suzanne wrote asking that his parents dissuade him from visiting with gifts. When Laure had found out about this she had turned on her mother and said, "I don't believe you want me to have suitors, *Maman*, you want to keep me beside you for ever!" She had sought her mother's forgiveness later on for this lapse in manners, but Suzanne, unusually for her, had given the matter much thought, questioning her motives, and wondering whether there could be some truth in this accusation. It was true that her marriage left her often alone, not knowing where Henri was, or who he might be with. She knew that he no longer found her physically attractive.

Their marriage in Mauritius had been an arranged one, but had worked well at first when she had youth on her side. Seventeen years later, Henri's position as a lawyer in the milieu of the French court brought him into contact with many of the important people of the day and there were beautiful women too. It could be said that Suzanne and Henri's marriage became an open one, but only on Henri's side.

"To keep by my side someone I love," thought Suzanne, "when without Laure I have nobody. Is that the sort of mother I am becoming?" There had also been the little baby Etienne, born in Mauritius a couple of years before Laure, who had died after only a few days of life. This loss had made the birth of Laure, a healthy baby who lived and loved her parents, a great happiness to be treasured. Suzanne had a circle of women friends in Paris it was true, but the married ones did not have wandering husbands, or if they did, their husbands were able to pull the wool over their eyes and still continue to appear happy with them, so that they did not complain. The single women, mostly widows, had a certain status in life either through their marriages, or because they were heiresses. Suzanne felt herself inferior because she was not Parisian born, but from a far-off colony, and unfortunately Henri's unfaithfulness was the subject of common gossip. She admitted to herself that she needed Laure's company and enjoyed having her by her side, to talk to or to listen to her playing her latest piano piece. Some of the women she knew had lapdogs they doted on. Suzanne shuddered to think that perhaps she was treating Laure in the same way as those ladies treated their pets, or that she might be making her daughter her prisoner.

Other than these unwelcome possible reasons, Suzanne's strong doubts about Douglas Wales' suitability as a candidate for Laure's hand in marriage, were mainly because he was not a Catholic, as she and Laure were. She knew that he was a Christian man. He took the prayers every evening at 9 pm and read from a small Bible which he appeared always to carry in a pocket. She had to admit that he looked very handsome at these services in his uniform of navy blue jacket with gold buttons and pale trousers.

Life in Mauritius when they arrived there was not going to be particularly easy, even surrounded by her relations. To be taken into the home of her sister would cause Suzanne to feel that she might be a burden, but owning a house of her own would, in the present circumstances, be well-nigh financially impossible. The best she could hope to do would be to rent one.

It had recently come to her knowledge that the ship Orient was in fact owned by Douglas Wales. The clergyman, Henry Manning, had informed her of this one day when they sat opposite each other at the dining table. It appeared that several years previously Douglas Wales had purchased the vessel from a Mr Stewart Marjoribanks. Working for the East India Company Douglas had risen in the ranks from midshipman to master in its chartered sailing vessels. When the East India Company ceased trading in 1836, turning their efforts instead to the administration of India, Douglas had continued to sail the oceans in his own ship, carrying cargoes from India, China and Australia and taking emigrants to start new lives in the colonies.

Henry Manning had told Suzanne that he had asked Douglas for the ship's history, and that this was when its present ownership had emerged. Suzanne's thoughts and feelings were beginning to confuse her. Douglas was so much older, he didn't speak fluent French, he was not a Catholic, but Douglas Wales was a man of means who owned a valuable asset. He was a man of the world, who had travelled to exciting places where he had met influential people, and he was obviously in love with her daughter who in turn seemed quite entranced by him. Ever the practical Frenchwoman, Suzanne was becoming less averse to the thought of a match between Laure and Douglas, although doubts remained.

"You are very flushed, Chérie" she said to Laure. "Have you a fever?"

Laure shook her head. "No, *Maman*, my forehead is quite cool," she said, "but Captain Wales told us the most exciting seafaring tale and it has made my heart beat fast." She sat down at the desk, and opened an English grammar book which John Browning had taken for her from the small library on the ship. She bent her head to read but found it difficult to concentrate. Why had she been so silly as to rush away like that? Captain Wales must have thought her very impetuous and possibly even impolite. The next day being Sunday, she decided that she would try to find an opportunity after the church service to apologize to him for her behaviour.

Douglas had returned to his duties soon after Laure rushed away. He had noticed her blushes and wondered at them. He had also noticed the admiration for him that shone from her bright eyes as she smiled at him. He felt extremely encouraged, and wished that he could declare his love for her, but he must wait until he had asked her mother for her daughter's hand in marriage.

The passengers in steerage

One of Douglas' tasks that morning was to speak to the passengers who had spent such an uncomfortable night during the storm. Before they had embarked in London, he had spoken to them and told them that all that could be done to make their voyage more tolerable would be done. He had emphasized the importance of co-operation and sticking to the rules of the ship. He had asked them to respect each other and to make sure everyone got their fair share of water and food. He told them that he would keep them informed of any points of interest such as exotic birds and fish to be seen and that they would be able to entertain themselves by singing, dancing or reciting, with himself and others on board as audience. They would be free to use the middle deck in groups of thirty to forty, for exercise and for the children to play.

Now however Douglas needed to make sure that those who were ill or had broken limbs were being cared for. There were two very small sick bays on the ship, one for men and one for women. In cases of infectious epidemics they would be less than useless as prevention of their spread, but there the ship's surgeon could set limbs and administer medicine in a way that would have been extremely difficult in the crowded steerage part of the ship.

Luckily the breaks in the limbs of the emigrants were clean fractures. The bone did not protrude through the skin. However at that time it could not be known how good a result would be obtained from setting them. Most of the fractures were of fingers and toes, with only the head injury needing the most care. One man had an ankle fracture, and a second man had a fracture of his right elbow. The surgeon was able to deal with all these patients with simple measures. A crutch was given to the man with the broken ankle after it had been tightly bound, bandages protecting the broken toes from further pain or injury. Several stitches were put in the head wound after it had been thoroughly cleansed and disinfected with iodine.

When Douglas went down the ladder into the emigrants' quarters he was welcomed by the passengers, some of whom cried out: "Thank you, Sir, for getting us safe after that storm," "God Bless you, Sir!" and "We owe our lives to you." Douglas held up his right hand to silence them and said, "It was my bounden duty to look after my passengers, and I am always aware that our Heavenly Father guides me. We shall have a special service tomorrow morning on the middle deck, and I hope as many of you as can do so will attend. Then in the evening of the next day, we must have a celebration, a dance perhaps. Please arrange a good band between you. There is a gentleman who plays the flute amongst us, and I will ask him to meet with your musicians. Some of my crew are past masters at playing accordions and they certainly know some good sea shanties." There was a roar of approval from the steerage passengers. Douglas left them excitedly discussing amongst themselves how the celebration would be arranged.

The two young couples

The two couples who were paying passengers had been quite unwell during the storm. Mr and Mrs Sedgewick and Mr and Mrs Walters had never been to sea before. They suffered considerably and when they finally made their appearance again in the dining saloon at teatime all four looked pale and wan. Anne Sedgewick told the steward that she would have tea – "but without milk, please. Just a slice of lemon." "That's a good idea," her husband Peter said and he passed her a plate of sweet biscuits, which his wife hastily waved away.

James and Agnes Walters were braver, and had tea with milk but refused the biscuits.

"The creaking noises that came from the ship's structure and what sounded like pistol shots when the timber settled – they were what frightened me most," said Anne to Agnes. "Oh yes, and the crashing of the waves against its sides and the dreadful moaning sound of the wind in the sails made me shudder," said Agnes. She went on: "James, in spite of being dreadfully unwell, tried to console me. How did your husband deal with it all?" Anne replied, "He started out being seemingly unconcerned, but when the sickness overcame him, he groaned in a most pitiful way for many hours!"

Their conversation was not heard by their husbands who were discussing the storm, the ship and its progress, and then on to the future and what they were proposing to do once they reached Australia. James Walters had a letter of introduction to a merchant who had gone out to Melbourne some years previously and set up a trading company there. "I have a tent I bought in London with me. I was advised that this would be the best way to spend the first few weeks in Australia, until I was able to find accommodation that suited our needs, or work to enable me to build a wooden house."

"You are fortunate," said Peter Sedgewick. "I know no one in Australia. I am simply hoping that there are vacancies for experienced accountants, but I am prepared to put my shoulder to the wheel and do anything at all that comes my way so that I can look after my wife, and make some sort of a home for us. It may be possible to purchase a tent once we arrive in Melbourne."

"Yes, indeed," said James, "but I have heard that prices are high for anything that might be useful to new settlers. They are high in every commodity I understand. I suppose it is human nature for those who came before us to wish to profit by their experience and make an extra sovereign or two." His companion agreed and said, "I am glad we came on this ship. The advertisement stressing the ship's strict punctuality meant that we were able to join Orient on a fixed day, thus avoiding the need to pay for accommodation in London while waiting to embark. We paid a reasonable sum to be brought to London from Sussex by carriage and were able to embark as soon as we arrived at the docks. Steam tugs were waiting to take us to the ship."

"We embarked at Plymouth," said James. "As my wife is with child, what decided us was the mention of an experienced surgeon on Orient, but the fixed day and reliable punctuality of departure was an added attraction."

Anne and Agnes then decided to climb the companion ladder up to the poop deck so that they could benefit from the fresh air and warmth of the sun. They found Laure already sitting there under a large awning that had been stretched over that part of the deck to provide shade. Laure was sitting with a book in her hand but she was looking out towards the horizon and not reading it. She greeted her fellow passengers with a smile and a few English words of welcome. "See, I am learning," she said, "but it is slow and I do not have the correct pronunciation."

"That will take time, my dear," said Anne, "and only by listening will it become apparent. You must however take into account the differences in the manner in which, for instance, Captain Wales and his officers speak to that of the crew members. It is a matter of birth you see – what station in life the speaker is from. In other words, it would not do for you to emulate the speech of a sailor or even of a petty officer."

"I should think not!" laughed Agnes. "Since a lot of the hands' conversation consists of oaths!"

"We have a church service on the middle deck at 10.30 tomorrow morning," said Henry Manning, who had joined them. "Captain Wales has asked me to take it, which I consider to be a great honour, because I have only recently been ordained. I believe the whole ship's company is expected to attend and it is customary for the sailors and everyone in steerage to put on their best clothes and uniforms."

"I am glad our trunks were brought up from the hold before the storm, so that we could take out more suitable clothing now that we are experiencing the tropical climate. Our English summers cannot be compared to the present weather conditions," Anne said. She had moved over to the side of the ship and was looking down at the sea below. Suddenly she cried out, "A whale! Look, look, it is tossing itself about and spouting!" Agnes, Henry and Laure joined her. "What a marvellous creature," said Laure. "See how it dives and comes up again as if it is playing with the ship!"

In order to be understood, she demonstrated by moving her right hand down and up again in imitation of the whale's antics. "'*Une baleine*'?" she said, turning to Henry, who replied, "A whale." Then, in French, she said to Henry, "The captain's name, is it anything to do with the *baleine*?" "No, because it is not spelled with an H," said Henry, "but he did tell an amusing story the other day when I was with him on deck. He said that when he was a child, and was taken to church in England, he and his brothers, whenever the psalm was sung in which the phrase 'All ye whales, praise ye the Lord' appears, all thought that this was a directive intended for their family only, and felt extremely proud to be so singled out. Captain Douglas said that he was quite disappointed when he found out later on that this was not the case."

Everyone laughed when he explained the joke in English, and the group spent a further hour enjoying the balmy air and the movement of the ship as she cut through the calm sea at quite a speed. In her foaming wake could be seen fish, amongst them flying fish, and birds dived down to make a meal of some of them. The flying fish were the size of small mackerel. They could be found sometimes in the early morning on the deck of the ship having been attracted during the night by the ship's lights. The birds that the ship's company had seen were Phaetons, Marlinespikes, Cape Pigeons and large black and white plumed birds known as Boatswains that were half the size of a chicken.

At 5 o'clock, the ship's bell sounded for dinner and all the cabin passengers, except for Suzanne Volpélière, sat down at the table. A veritable feast was served to them. There was soup, a choice of roast mutton or poultry, plenty of vegetables and for pudding a tart made of preserved fruit.

Laure asked the steward to put soup and bread, and a small glass of whisky and water on a tray to take to her mother. She would go to see if her mother had been able to take any nourishment once the dinner was over.

Douglas did not dine with his passengers. He had his log to write up, and various documents to read. He dined separately with his first mate and the surgeon that evening. There were matters relating to the steerage passengers injured in the storm to discuss and also a disciplinary problem relating to one of the emigrants who had been found the worse for drink and who had started a fight with another man. The passengers in steerage had begun to take sides, and those for the man who was being punished were coming up against those against him in a way that might well have started a riot.

The cause of the fight was a woman, wife of the man now in irons whose husband accused the other man of leering at her in a suggestive fashion. Douglas ordered two of the constables to go to the 'tween deck and tell the emigrants that, if there was any further trouble, more of them would be taken into custody for the duration of the journey and that the captain had ordered that firearms be loaded with shot. An uprising in steerage would harm the necessary smooth running of the ship, as the crew would be distracted, so the seriousness of the situation needed to be firmly stated.

Luckily the potential trouble makers were in the minority, and most of the emigrants were either taking the air on the main deck, or gathering in groups to discuss the forthcoming service the next morning, and the dance the following evening. Clean clothing was taken out of bags and boxes. Shoes were cleaned. On deck some of the women washed their children's hair and hung washed clothes out to dry. Excitement was in the air.

Down below, those passengers who could play instruments - the fiddle, the accordion, the pennywhistle

- began some dance tunes. A young man broke into a folksong, and others joined in. Several young women began to dance in an empty corner of the 'tween deck to the tune of a fiddle played by another, older, man. Small children ran towards the music, clapping their hands happily. The whole atmosphere was lightened and all went about their business in a more hopeful and contented frame of mind.

The Church Service

Music was provided for the service by an accordion and a violin played by two sailors and a clarinet played by one of the ship's officers.

All present were in their best garments, very clean even if shabby. Jane and her son, whom Laure had met on the middle deck, stood proudly with Jane's husband George in the congregation. The little boy wore a tunic his mother had made, over white trousers, and she had embroidered an anchor at the neck of the tunic. Laure smiled at them from her place with the other cabin passengers, and they returned her smile. She too was standing, but a chair had been brought for Suzanne who was glad to be seated as she was still feeling the effects of the storm. The officers were very smart in their navy blue jackets with gold buttons, as was the captain, in his dress uniform.

To start the service Hymn No. 371 'Almighty Father, hear our cry as o'er the trackless deep we roam' was played and sung. Douglas had decided not to include Hymn No. 370 'Eternal Father strong to save', because the last line of each verse ended with the words "For those in peril on the sea". He thought that this might cause his passengers to believe that they were constantly in danger. In spite of all their past suffering, the whole ship's company raised their voices and the resulting sound seemed capable of reaching up into the sky to the heavens themselves.

Henry Manning led the prayers, starting with one thanking God for having brought Orient safely through the storm. The congregation all voiced a fervent "Amen".

After the service, the passengers from steerage enjoyed freedom to exercise in supervised groups on the middle deck before their midday meal. That morning, the ship's cook had agreed to bake several large fruit cakes for them to enjoy at the dance. There were sounds of music being played in various parts of the ship, as the musicians practised the folksongs and dances they would entertain their fellow travellers with at the coming dance. Already quite a number of people were raising their voices in song and little children hopped and jumped to the music. Laure, who had gone up to the poop deck and was sitting under the awning thought it was a most merry sound.

Laure was hoping that Captain Douglas would also be ascending the ladder and onto the poop-deck, as several of the ship's officers had done so and were enjoying the companionship of each other and of the cabin passengers. Sure enough, before too long, Laure saw Douglas coming towards her. He bowed from the waist and said in French but with a strong English accent, "Mademoiselle Laure, may I sit beside you?"

"*Certainement*," replied Laure, "and, Captain Wales, I owe you an apology for leaving the saloon so hurriedly last evening."

With varying degrees of success, Laure was able to make Douglas understand what she meant. She had the English/French dictionary that the schoolmaster had lent her and at one point their two heads came close together as they searched for suitable translation of words. Douglas was able to reassure Laure that no offence had been taken at her abrupt departure. In clumsy French he told her that he had feared that she might have been taken ill and had been very glad to find that this was not so.

"When we disembark at Mauritius, will you take on other passengers?" Laure asked him.

"Not emigrant passengers," he replied, "but there may be several cabin passengers to be taken home to Australia, and I shall also carry a cargo of sugar from Mauritius."

Douglas was revelling in the fact that he and Laure were able to sit together and converse. Their efforts in each other's language boded well for the future he thought, and once more he was strongly tempted to give Laure a hint of the seriousness of his intentions towards her. However he decided against this because he did not want to put a foot wrong where her mother was concerned, and he would need to broach the subject with Suzanne before doing so with Laure. Everything he had noticed about Laure in the weeks that he had observed her made him realize more strongly how he admired her character and her courage. Not many eighteen-year-old girls would endure such a journey without making any complaint. She had shown herself competent in looking after her mother and he liked the fact that she was interested in the steerage passengers and even asked intelligent questions about the running of the ship.

Douglas hoped that he was not deluding himself into believing that such a young girl as Laure really was attracted to him. The only way to find out was to go to her mother and declare his intentions. Only if she accepted him could he then propose to Laure and finally know what was in her heart.
Suzanne was able to come to the dinner table that evening, looking pale, but putting on a brave face and enjoying some soup. Laure was very excited about the dance and had spent some time before dinner deciding on a suitable dress. For once Suzanne did not try to damp her daughter's enthusiasm. She resigned herself to "what would be, would be".

The Dance on Board

The dance on board would take place on the poop deck and the main deck. For convention's sake the steerage passengers would dance on the middle deck and the cabin passengers, being fewer, would dance on the poop deck.

Laure decided eventually on the apricot coloured silk dress she had worn for the presentation of her diploma at the Paris Conservatoire a year earlier. It had large puffed sleeves that tapered at the wrists and, although Laure felt that it was not cut low enough at the neck, the material it was made from and the colour were more suitable than any other dress she had brought with her. Sighing, she said to herself, "I wish it made me look a little more grown up," and she regarded herself critically in the mirror as she brushed her dark hair.

"My face is too round," she thought, "and my cheeks are too pink. To be really interesting, a lady should be pale with high cheekbones. That is how they are described in the novels I have read." She found the jet necklace that had been a birthday present from her father, and was pleased with its effect against the warm apricot of the gown. Her hair was parted in the middle and drawn back into a chignon. Small dangling jet earrings and elbow length black gloves completed her toilette. In her hand she carried a black fan.

"How do I look, *Maman*?" she asked Suzanne. "Do you think I could have a little powder on tonight?"

"No, chérie" Suzanne replied. "While you are young and your skin is healthy, why cover it up?" But she agreed that Laure could put a little rouge on the tip of a finger and rub it on her lips.

Suzanne was also going to the dance in her role as chaperone. She thought it would be enjoyable to be on deck and listening to music, and her health was beginning to return. She was looking forward to the refreshments she had heard Douglas mention.

Anne Sedgwick and Agnes Walters and their husbands were the first cabin passengers to arrive at the dance, but already the ship's officers and the captain were there to greet them, and the band immediately struck up with a polka. The young couples and some of the emigrants on the main deck started to dance.

When Suzanne and Laure arrived, Douglas immediately came towards them and asked if he could have the pleasure of the next dance with Laure. It was a waltz and when Laure felt Douglas' right arm around her waist, and when she placed her left hand lightly on his right shoulder, she experienced a feeling of calm certainty that here she belonged, here was her destiny. Douglas, too, her right hand held lightly in his left, told himself that he felt somehow at peace with Laure in his arms, and knew that she was all that he wanted.

It was a pretty scene with the dark sky full of twinkling stars, and the oil lamps surrounding the decks casting their light on the happy faces of the dancers and those of the musicians too. A certain Mr Liddiard, who played the clarinet, had been allowed to join the band in spite of the fact that he had sorely irritated the cabin passengers when he had decided on several occasions to practise his instrument whilst the captain was reading prayers at 9 pm. It had been touch and go whether he would be punished when he refused to refrain from doing this and became somewhat belligerent. However he had been persuaded to behave.

When the waltz ended, Douglas led Laure back to where her mother and other passengers were sitting enjoying glasses of wine or lemonade and sampling some of the delicacies that had been made for the occasion. John Browning, who had been sitting beside Agnes Walters, who was sipping a glass of lemonade, rose to his feet when he saw Laure approaching and said, "Miss Laure, you look very well in that colour gown. It compliments your dark hair." Laure was shyly pleased at this, and thanked him. "Will you be my partner for the next dance?" John then asked her, and Laure said she would be delighted. To his own surprise Douglas found himself discomfited by the young man's attentions to Laure. He thought himself to be a man of the world and a very sensible person, and here he was suddenly feeling annoyed that another man, one younger than he, was paying Laure compliments which she seemed happy about.

"Do not fill your dance card up completely, *Mademoiselle*," he said to Laure. "I should like to partner you for at least three dances." Laura smiled her agreement, and Douglas turned on his heel and went to join a group of officers and guests nearby. Laure found it sad that the steerage passengers were segregated from the cabin passengers and were only allowed on the main deck. As she and John Browning circled round, she looked down at the deck below and saw the young woman, Jane from steerage, dancing with her little boy. "Oh how sweet that is," Laure said to John; "he is having the time of his life." Indeed, little Georgy was jumping, holding on to his mother's hands, in good time with the music. Henry Manning had joined the band and was playing a merry folkdance on his flute. Jane's husband George was standing watching his wife and son, and tapping his foot in time to the dance.

"Another dance for me please, *Mademoiselle*," John Browning requested, and he and Laure joined several other couples to make up a quadrille. John was an accomplished dancer, noted Douglas, who was watching them intently, and Laure was obviously enjoying herself, smiling at her partner when she passed him in the dance. Douglas determined to claim her for the next dance, but he was called away to deal with a shipboard matter just as the quadrille ended. A drunken crew member had been insubordinately refusing to go to his duties and was obstreperous enough to have had to be put in irons and confined until he sobered up.

Laure looked for Douglas when John led her back to her seat, and her heart sank when she could not see him. A break in the dancing followed, and an emigrant man entertained the company by singing a ballad, accompanied by a crew member on the accordion. Little Georgy, his mother and father had found a comfortable place to sit on the deck with their plates of refreshments, the most appreciated of which was the fruit cake. There was ale for the man and lemonade for the child and his mother. This little family, the Harrises, had left behind them parents and grandparents in the West of England, and did not expect ever to see them again. The adults were therefore often feeling sad, but tonight they cast care away and joined in the fun.

"That young lady with dark hair," said George Harris to his wife, "she is the French lady who spoke to you when you were at the brazier on deck, isn't she?" "Yes," replied Jane. "She seemed very pleasant and interested in me and our child. She insisted on coming down to see what we were all doing on the main deck. I think Captain Wales is taken with her, and I believe she likes him too."

"She's a might young for him, isn't she?" her husband said. "She looks not long out of school."

"I was seventeen when you and I married," Jane said.

"But I was young too," George replied. "Captain Wales must be over thirty."

"Sometimes the happiest of marriages can be when the husband is quite a lot older than his wife," said Jane. "My father is fifteen years older than my mother and, even though their life has been so hard, they have been contented together." The thought of her parents being so far away now momentarily saddened her once more, but she put on a brave face and enjoyed what she could of the happy time available.

The band struck up again with a gallop and Jane, George and their son all joined in the dance together, with the child sitting on his father's shoulders and crowing with delight at being so high and being able to look up into the sails of the ship, which were billowing with a strong wind behind them, sending the ship forward with speed.

Some of the emigrants were looking forward to taking their turn sleeping on deck as the weather was so warm. A rota had been made up and groups of about twenty five steerage passengers were able to benefit from the cool of the night. This continued until everyone who wished it had had a turn at experiencing a more comfortable night.

John Browning, who was dancing with Laure for the second time, said to her, "Would you care to join me when I give a lesson to some of the children tomorrow on deck? I shall be helping them with their reading, and you might find it a useful way of increasing your English vocabulary."

"That would be delightful," said Laure. "I am improving a little, but there is a long way to go." She spoke in English.

"You definitely have improved," said John, "and in only a few weeks! Your sentences flow better now. I can tell that you have studied well."

Laure, although thoroughly enjoying the music and steps of the dance, was still hoping to see Douglas back amongst them, and she was pleased when he did return. He stood near Suzanne and was watching the dancers. As soon as the dance was over, he claimed Laure for the next one, a mazurka this time, and she once again felt completely at home in his arms.

Their steps in the mazurka matched perfectly. They made a handsome couple. Laure told Douglas about the schoolmaster's invitation to attend a class the next day. Douglas was against this mainly because of the danger of close contact with emigrant children, leading to the possibility that any infection they might be carrying would be passed on to Laure. He also admitted to himself that he would prefer Laure not to have too much contact with the schoolmaster as he had observed that John Browning was as taken with Laure as Douglas himself was.

When he gave Laure his first reason against the idea, she said that surely if the lessons took place on deck, and not in the 'tween deck, there would less need to fear infection. Douglas was unable to refute this, and feeling unable to mention his wish that she did not have too much to do with John, the matter was decided. Laure said that she would be chaperoned by either Agnes or Anne. She felt sure she could persuade one or other of them to fulfil this duty. She gave herself up to the enjoyment of the dance, delighted when one of Douglas' steps culminated in him kneeling on one knee before her.

"Captain Wales," she said then, "let us have the third dance immediately after this one. Otherwise you may be called away again and not return before the end of the dance." It was the custom at that time that if a young lady favoured one of her partners at a ball she could make him aware of this by dancing three times with him and then, at a future date, returning to him her dance card, which would indicate that she was accepting him as a suitor. Douglas therefore was delighted by her remark and momentarily tightened his arm around her waist, looking down at her with a broad smile. When that dance ended he stayed by Laure's side while the band was tuning up for the next one and, as soon as the first chord of the schottische was struck, he led her onto the floor. At the end of the schottische he took Laure's dance card and he gravely wrote his name three times in it before handing it back to her. They then rejoined the other members of the party for refreshments.

Meanwhile the Harris family had found a safe corner nearby on the deck by some coiled ropes, where they laid their tired son to sleep on a piece of sacking. Keeping in a position on the deck from which they could constantly see him, they danced together. George Harris wondered to himself whether, his wife being known to Laure, Laure might be prevailed upon to ask Captain Douglas whether he might consider putting in a good word for George in his search for employment once they reached Australia. If there were to be work to do straight away on arrival, life would be much easier. George had worked on the land in England. He was strongly built, young and prepared to give his all to an employer. He was literate and was attending the classes on the ship to improve himself. George decided to discuss this with Jane later on that night. Why, perhaps Jane could obtain employment also. She was a good seamstress.

At the end of the dance Laure knew that she had even deeper feelings now for Douglas than before and the way he had looked at her was a sure indication that he reciprocated these. The band struck up with 'Auld Lang Syne', and there were some tears from the assembled company when they thought of all those they had parted from, but 'God Save the Queen' robustly ended the evening, and everyone retired to their beds and bunks exhausted but happy.

The Mutiny

The next day dawned fair, and on deck early in the morning Jane was making coffee for George at the brazier near the mainmast when she noticed a group of seamen apparently arguing with two officers. She became troubled when the men's voices became raised. One officer left the scene but soon returned with Captain Wales and other officers came to his side quickly. The crew members were questioned as to the reason for their belligerence, and one of them replied that until a certain Jasper Jones, who had refused to go to his duties and had been confined in a cabin in irons, was released his fellow shipmates would not obey orders and carry out their own duties. This group of seamen were also put into confinement then by the ship's officers.

Jane, being close enough to witness all this, quickly removed the coffee pot from the brazier, and went with it towards the companionway to the 'tween deck where she was joined by several other emigrants who had also become nervous about the situation. At that point Douglas shouted out, "All assisted emigrants to go below immediately," and they all obeyed and took themselves hastily down to their quarters.

When Jane reached her husband, who was sitting at the long table between the two-tiered bunks in the steerage quarter, he looked up from the writing he was engaged in and asked why everyone was returning so hastily below deck.

"Ah! That is very serious," he said softly, when he heard what was happening above them. "A mutiny on board such a ship as ours is extremely dangerous as, if the crew refuse to work the sails and the officers are busy dealing with their grievances, the ship could go off course into more perilous waters." He kept his voice down for the sake of Georgy, who was sitting at the table beside him.

Jane nodded and sat down beside the little boy who had been playing with a wooden top he balanced on the table. She bent and gave him a kiss and said, "It won't be long Georgy before I can go up again and make you some porridge." She turned to a metal box amongst the possessions on their bunk, opened it and took out a small piece of fruit cake, saved from the dance. Georgy was very pleased to receive it, and was soon enjoying this piece of luxury.

The rest of the many emigrants were clustering together, anxiously discussing the drama going on above them. Once again they experienced fear, and the reality of their situation on board a wooden sailing ship in the middle of the ocean, some of whose crew were at loggerheads with its captain and his officers, gave rise to much trepidation.

On deck, to the dismay of the officers, the rest of the ship's company, greatly outnumbering them all, joined in the fray, stating in a very mutinous fashion that until **all** their shipmates were immediately released, they too would do no duties. Several of the ringleaders then enquired in a loud and insolent manner if they were **all** therefore going to be put in irons and confined. Captain Wales tried to reason with them, stating the case for Jones' and his shipmates' punishment, saying that disobeying the orders of the chief mate was putting the ship in danger and could not be tolerated. Douglas then ordered them to muster in the stern of the ship and think all this over while he consulted with the officers as to the best way to deal with this alarming situation. It was decided to ask one from the first group of seamen if he would, having thought things over, now return to his duties. Douglas chose the ringleader, Bob Styles, and posed the question to him. Looking around for the approbation of the rest of the ship's crew, Bob Styles replied loudly and forcibly, "No!"

At that, without ado, Douglas and his officers seized the man and gave him one dozen strokes of the lash. At the end of this punishment Bob Styles stated that he **would** obey orders, the pain of the punishment being such a severe one. But he remained angry.

Then Douglas asked the rest of the crew in turn and by name if they would also go to their duties, and they all answered in the affirmative. Douglas and his officers were suitably relieved by this. He called the watch and arranged for the cleaning of the deck, which was dreadfully blood stained from Bob Styles' lashing.

All was not resolved however as the captain and officers had thought. Only a few minutes elapsed before Douglas heard a tremendous noise coming from the cabin where the prisoners had been confined. There issued forth dreadful oaths and shouted demands to be released immediately, or else…….! The threats were particularly directed towards Douglas himself. He and three more officers went down, and on opening the cabin door Douglas was immediately faced with the alarming sight of Jasper Jones brandishing a large knife at him. The prisoner yelled, "Who dares to pass through this door now!"

As an officer made to take the knife away from him, Jones raised it and was bringing it down to stab Douglas, but the latter gripped his wrist to prevent this. The first mate then wrested the knife from the seaman's hand.

All the prisoners were in a furiously mutinous frame of mind by then, and Douglas and his officers were hard put to control them. Even when they had succeeded, a certain Joshua Grimes made an attempt to stab the first mate, succeeding only in cutting his trousers before he was lashed to the deck. This group of ten mutinous seamen were then put into irons and confined.

Fortunately for all on board the rest of the crew had returned to their duties, and the ship sailed on having escaped the dire possibility of going off course or worse.

Douglas returned to the quarterdeck to make sure the helmsmen were tackling their duty satisfactorily, after which he joined the officers in the Great Cabin where discussion took place as to what should be done with the prisoners.

"I am well minded to carry them to Port Phillip and deliver them to the civil authorities there," Douglas told the officers. "However in spite of the dreadful threats they made that were directed towards me the entire time, I shall not make such a decision immediately."

His officers were not wholeheartedly in agreement with Douglas, feeling that the matter could only be resolved by the civil authorities on arrival in Australia, but his word being law they could only accept his present decision.

Laure's reaction to the Mutiny

While the mutiny was taking place, Suzanne, Laure and the other cabin passengers, who had been taking the air on the poop deck, had also been advised by an officer to go down to the saloon, and did so immediately.

While feeling sure that Douglas would know exactly what to do, and that he would deal with the situation in the best way possible, Laure was unable not to feel anxious about his welfare. She had observed that there were many more crew members than there were officers. She prayed that the officers would not be outnumbered as had happened in the past to captains of navy vessels and masters of trading ships. Her grandfather had been a ship owner in Marseilles, and her father Henri had told her exciting stories of mutinies and piracy and such seafaring tales. She was worried that Douglas might be wounded or worse, and then it was that, clear as a bell in her mind, came the words "I love him" and "I believe he loves me. We are meant to be together. No other man can ever mean as much to me as he does."

Suzanne had begun to weep from fear, so Laure had to stop her thoughts running away and turn from them to comfort her mother. All the cabin passengers had tried to busy themselves with cards or reading or chatting quietly. Henry Manning had read his Bible and then offered up a prayer on behalf of them all. Sitting beside her mother Laure had held her hand and gradually Suzanne had composed herself.

Unfortunately the thundering footsteps on the deck above as the crew moved forward mutinously, and then all went aft, returning to deliver their intentions to continue to mutiny, followed by the unmistakable sounds of the dreadful punishment of lashings, had been all too easily heard by everyone in the saloon. The passengers however had been on the whole dignified in their endurance.

After the dreadful noise had abated and an officer came to inform the saloon passengers that all was now well and the mutiny over, Laure made the sudden decision that she must find Douglas Wales in order to see for herself that he was safe. All caution flew to the wind. She simply knew that it was imperative that she followed her heart regardless of the consequences, and, telling her mother that she needed to go to their cabin now but would return swiftly, she made her way to the deck looking anxiously about her for Douglas. He was not present. The crew were going about their duties. The helmsmen were at the wheel and the 2nd and 3rd mates were keeping watch. When they saw the young French girl coming towards them, William Maurice, the 3rd mate, came quickly to meet her. In a not too successful attempt to control her anxiety Laure asked him where Captain Wales was. "He is in his cabin, *Mademoiselle*," William Maurice answered.

Before he could say more, Laure had descended the ladder to the main deck and was running towards the Great Cabin, clutching her skirt up in both hands so that it did not impede her progress, and not noticing that her hair had escaped its fastenings and was streaming behind her. Startled sailors, and male emigrants cleaning the deck, stood hastily aside to prevent her cannoning into them as she ran past. Geese, ducks and hens cackled loudly in alarm as she rushed past their coops.

Douglas, alerted by loud knocking on his cabin door, opened it, and Laure fell towards him, completely out of breath. Douglas caught her in his arms and felt Laure's arms go round his neck and tighten there. Her face was pressed into his chest, and she was sobbing.

Douglas, horrified that Laure had put herself and, indeed, him in such a compromising situation cried out, "My dear, my dear! Whatever has come over you?" and led the weeping girl to a chair, taking the one next to her. "I have not closed the door," he said; "you must not be alone with me here and you should not have come alone. Please tell me why you have done so and why you are so distressed." He looked at Laure, whose hair was loose and fell over her shoulders in complete disarray. Teardrops had landed on the front of her dress leaving marks in the material and the tears were still spilling from her eyes. She put her hands over her face and spoke in French, her English having completely deserted her.

Straining to hear and understand, Douglas heard her say: "I did not know if you had come out of the dreadful mutiny without injury. I was so afraid, but I am weeping now because I feel relief that you are safe." Douglas was very touched by these words and, disregarding any qualms he might have had as to the wisdom of such an action, he took her hand and kissed it. Laure looked into his face with an expression of such radiant affection that it was all Douglas could do not to take her into his arms and kiss her. But he allowed himself only to say to Laure: "I am touched beyond belief that you care for me so much that you could rush to my side as you did. You must know that I also care for you, more than I can say, but you are very young and need to remain in the care of your mother who has charge over you at present."

The conventions of the day required a young woman when she "came out" in society at the age of eighteen to remain under the care of her mother for three years until she came of age at twenty one. Douglas also knew that he must behave in the most circumspect manner or run the risk of alienating Suzanne Volpélière.

Douglas drew a clean handkerchief from his pocket and gave it to Laure, who patted her face with it, drying up her tears. She started to laugh softly as she began to gather up her unruly locks, and, because some of the hairpins had fallen out in her flight to Douglas, she simply tied her hair back with two of the clasps that had not fallen as she ran. "I must look a fright," she said in English, and Douglas simply shook his head and very quietly said, "No." Then he went on: "Now I must take you back to your mother," and he started to rise to his feet.

"Wait please…." Laure beseeched him, and she drew out from her sleeve the dance card in which Douglas had written his name three times. "I should like to return this to you now," she told Douglas, who took it from her and tucked it into his breast pocket.

"I wish I was older," said Laure. "It is exceedingly tiresome that I am not."

Douglas gave her his arm, and together they left the Great Cabin. Douglas saw Laure to the companion ladder and waited until she disappeared down towards the saloon. Then he turned away and walked back to his cabin, thinking to himself that he must be the happiest man alive. How difficult it had been for him not to embrace her! Now she had formally accepted him as a suitor when she returned her dance card to him. It was much too soon, Douglas told himself, to speak to Suzanne and announce his intentions. A serious courtship needed a suitable environment in which a gentleman would visit the young lady at home with bouquets of flowers and perform all the other niceties required of a suitor on dry land. It seemed foolish to speak to Suzanne straight away without giving thought to the reasons that would most probably be put forward by that lady against a match between Laure and himself. Douglas decided to bide his time.

Plans of the Harris family

Later that day, when the Harris family were sitting as comfortably as possible in their bunk, the child Georgy in the lower bunk which he shared with some of the family's possessions, Jane asked her husband what he had been writing when she had joined him at the start of the mutiny. George Harris drew out from his pocket a letter.

"It is a letter to Captain Wales, enquiring if he might put in a good word for us, helping us to find work in Australia," George told her. "I did wonder though, when the trouble had started, if the happenings on deck would prevent us arriving in that country after all!"

"A terrible thought, dearest!" Jane said. "After all the sacrifices we made to make this journey, how dreadful it would be if they were all for naught and we were lost at sea."

"Will you read what I have put down so far?" asked George, after giving her hand a squeeze to stop the tears that were gathering in her eyes. Jane nodded, and George passed the letter to her. She read it slowly.

To Captain Wales

Sir
I hope you will do me the honour of reading these words. I would be much obliged if so. Me and wife Jane are hard workers. I tilled the land in the West Country from aged 10. I ploughed, planted seed, harvested crops, cut wood, saw to cattle and horses. My Jane learned sewing from her mother. She cooks well and keeps a fair kitchen garden. She sews our clothes, repairing the old garments and making new. Both me and wife can read and write.

If there is a person known to you on the ship, or in the new country, who might offer employment, we can promise you that you would have no cause to regret putting us forward. In the hopes that you will consider my request,

I remain your faithful servant and passenger in the 'tween deck.

George Harris

Jane turned her face to his and said, "That is very good writing and spelling, my dear. You begin respectfully and with gratitude and you put our case without seeming pitiable. How shall you deliver it to the captain?"

Her husband replied, "I believe that *Mademoiselle*, having spoken kindly to you at the brazier, and having greeted us all at the dance, will be the best person to receive the letter and could be requested to pass it to

Captain Wales. Perhaps she would help our cause by adding her own opinion of us."

Jane agreed, and tucked the letter into her apron pocket, determined to deliver it to Laure as soon as she could.

George Harris' letter is given to Laure

Several days later, as Laure was exercising with Agnes and Anne on the poop deck, she saw Jane Harris hanging out some washing on the rigging below. A large tabby cat was winding itself round Jane's ankles. The sun was brilliant that day, and Orient seemed to gallop along, dipping her bows a little way down before breasting the next wave the sea tossed up. There was a good breeze, and under the awning on the poop deck the temperature was quite tolerable.

Shooing the cat away Jane turned and looked upwards to where Laure and her companions were looking down at the middle deck. On seeing her, Laure immediately went to the top of the ladder and Jane approached it with quick steps.

"Miss, it is good to see you. I have a request to make if you please," she said.

Laure understood and said, "What is it? Please tell me."

Jane put her hand in her pocket and took out George's letter to Douglas. "May I come up?" She made to put her foot on the bottom rung of the ladder and without hesitation Laure came down to her level and took the letter from her.

"It is for Captain Wales," the young woman told Laure. "My husband and I wonder if, as you have some knowledge of us, you might be so kind as to put in a good word for us. We are seeking work in Australia and perhaps the good captain will know of a possible employer there."

Laure was able to understand the request after Jane repeated some phrases and words, and she was happy to assure her that she would give the letter to Douglas at the first opportunity. This she did at dinner that very day, reminding Douglas that she had seen and spoken to Jane Harris when walking with him along the middle deck.

Douglas, after reading the letter at the dinner table, handed it to James Walters to read. When James looked up at him enquiringly, Douglas said, "Might you and your wife need assistance when you reach the colony?"

"My funds will only allow me to offer lodgings - provided I can acquire a second tent - and food until I find work myself," James replied. "I would be glad to offer this if it was of some assistance to them, particularly because I know Agnes would be very happy to have some female support, especially when our child is born. The man of the family could engage in pursuing employment himself."

"That would be a great help to them," said Laure.

Douglas then said, "I know of several merchants and owners of cattle stations in Williamstown which is not far from Port Phillip, and I have contact with various settlers in Melbourne." He saw the pleasure these words gave to Laure and went on: "I consider it enterprising of this man to write to me, and he writes well. I shall be glad to mention this family for work once we arrive."

It was agreed that Douglas would write to George Harris with this information. Laure was able the next morning to pass Douglas' reply to Jane when they met on deck and wreathed in smiles Jane thanked Laure. As soon as she had finished cooking she took the letter down to George, who was hard at work with other emigrants cleaning the 'tween deck so that every emigrant could leave their bunk and sit at the table for the first meal of the day. Both he and Jane now felt far more hopeful about the life ahead of them in a strange land, knowing that there was the chance of lodging and work for the family.

For Laure this was yet another indication of the kindness of the man she knew she loved.

The Lesson on Deck

That same morning John Browning, the schoolmaster, rang a bell to announce the start of the class for emigrant children between the ages of five and fourteen. There were about sixty of these. The commotion in the 'tween deck as they all, if old enough, tidied themselves up and, if too young, allowed their mothers to wipe their faces and noses, and comb their hair, whilst all talking at the tops of their voices, was easily heard by the whole ship. It was a wonderful opportunity to be out in the open air even if it meant sitting quietly listening to the schoolmaster and doing what he told them to do, so they were all pleasurably excited.

First of all they had to be inspected by the schoolmaster, as was the custom. It was his duty to report to the captain or the doctor if a child was found to be very unkempt or unwell. If the first, they would be taken down to their parents for further tidying up. If they were unwell, Dr Grant would suggest remedies and see that they were carried out. As it was impossible for more than a few passengers in steerage to be isolated owing to the limited space in the sick bays, disease spread fast. Measles was the most serious threat to the emigrants as its spread caused fatalities, particularly in children. Children suffering from dysentery were sent back down to their bunks with rudimentary medicine from the doctor. It was the best anyone could do at that time.

As had been prearranged, Laure, accompanied by Anne Sedgewick, joined John at the beginning of the class and both young women sat on wooden chairs next to him and opposite the rows of children, who were sitting cross-legged on the deck, the older ones at the back and the youngest in the front. John had set up a blackboard and he was engaged in writing the alphabet in large letters. Each child had a slate on which they were copying the letters. John asked the older children to help the younger ones in this task. In this way the time was occupied for the older children who might otherwise, being able to write, have become bored and restless.

Words were written next by the schoolmaster, simple three letter ones. The younger pupils were encouraged to copy them and then read them out, as many as were able, together.

John then moved on to writing short sentences, asking for volunteers to read them out. Laure did not come forward for this purpose because she was afraid that her accent might cause her embarrassment if it engendered hilarity from the children. She simply copied down the sentences in her notebook.

"*Mademoiselle*," John said, "please try to translate the sentences into French and write that down." Laure began to do so, and thus the first hour of the lesson was taken up with writing and reading. The second hour was for numbers, addition and subtraction, starting with the simplest sums at first. After the youngest pupils had been helped to add two and two together and so on, several of the older pupils were asked by John to return the youngest children to their families in the 'tween deck, and while this was happening John put some sums on the blackboard which the older children were asked to complete when they all were present.

Laure listened to John's tuition in English and took note of it all, speaking the numbers in that language under her breath. She felt that the two hours were very well spent and thought John was an excellent tutor. He was so patient. She had noticed George Harris slipping in at the back of the class once the tuition became more suitable for him. She waited to speak to him when the class finished.

George was a handsome young man with auburn hair and beard. He was of middle height with broad shoulders and he was tidily dressed in brown trousers with a black leather belt around his waist, and above that a grey shirt and loosely knotted handkerchief at the neck. In order to be as well dressed as possible he had worn a loose jacket which, although obviously not new, was spotlessly clean. He recognized Laure and inclined his head slightly.

"Thank you, Miss, for your help in delivering my letter to Captain Wales," he said.

"I hope it will result in your finding a good position in Australia," she replied in English.

"Thank you, Miss," he responded and went on: "My wife was afraid of coming on this journey, but now she is comforted by the thought of a possible opening for me at least."

They parted company, George down to the crowded 'tween deck and Laure back to the cabin she shared with her mother to prepare herself for the midday meal.

Crossing the Line

Orient had been sailing now for four weeks and the next morning, there having been a good wind all through the night, it was clear to Douglas Wales that she would cross the equatorial line before sunset. At breakfast he asked all the cabin passengers to make a donation, enough to provide the crew with some tobacco and grog, and all the emigrants with some punch for the men and negus, (hot sweetened wine and water) for the women. A time was given, 3 o'clock, when Orient would be over the line. Some of the emigrants were very anxious to see this line about which so much had been said, and one of the crew laid a hair across the half-transparent, half-mirror horizon glass at the front of a telescope. Until he was discovered doing this, he was charging so much per head for a sight of this line that was more hirsute than equatorial and managed to collect a considerable amount before being prevented. Those he had deceived, who had been pleased to be able to discern the line so distinctly, were enraged when they realized that they had been tricked. Money was returned forthwith without too many scuffles.

Douglas, after the midday meal in the saloon, said that the health of all on board his ship should be drunk and told his passengers that, as Orient was now in the south latitude, there should be a celebration so a variety of songs were sung, accompanied by a few bowls of punch. The passengers (Laure the most enthusiastically but not immodestly) then drank Douglas' health in return and made speeches of a loyal and patriotic nature. The afternoon was spent exceedingly agreeably.

Soon after dark when it was comparatively quiet, a gruff and stern voice seemed to hail Orient from the water under her bows. A general rush forward took place to ascertain where the voice came from and it was discovered that Neptune (a sailor suitably attired and carrying a trident) had got a footing on the bowsprit, as had some of his assistants, and the numerous spectators were immediately saluted with bucketsful of his native element, which caused much fun and laughter although many were drenched and dripping. They all moved away from Father Neptune and he and his attendants sank, it was supposed, quietly into his own watery home.

Later in the evening a large number of emigrants congregated on the middle deck and there was some dancing and singing amongst them. Although the band was not as large as the one for the previous dance on board, and this time it was only the emigrants who danced, they had an appreciative audience on the poop deck, some of whom enjoyed singing choruses along with them.

John Browning's thoughts about Laure

In his cabin that night John Browning wrote to his sister Emily describing to her the lesson on deck that morning. He told her of the young French girl who had been pleased to attend and had done her best to profit from the class so that she could improve her English. As he wrote he found himself remembering many things that had appealed to him about Laure, her bent head over her notebook, the sun shining on her dark hair, the charming smile she gave him when he spoke to her, the attention she paid to all he was teaching and her obvious enjoyment in watching the little children as they struggled with their writing.

"I find myself very taken with her, he wrote. *It is her character that brings about her beauty. She does not*

have classical features as such, but her eyes are so bright, and she has a small nose and rosy cheeks…. "

John wondered if Laure would welcome it if he continued to try to interest her in himself and his work. She had asked him, when the passengers and Captain Wales were in the saloon after dinner and were enjoying celebrating the crossing of the line, whether he had brothers or sisters, and whereabouts his family home was in England. John had said that he would show her daguerreotype portraits of his parents and sister and brother the next morning. Laure had said that she would look forward to this and it had been arranged that they would meet on the poop deck after breakfast if it was fine weather or in the saloon if it was not. John wrote of this to his sister, ended the letter "Your affectionate brother", and blew out the candle before getting into his bunk. All candles had to be extinguished at 9 pm so it was very much early to bed and early to rise in Orient.

Death and burial of an infant

In the early hours of the next day an infant of a few months who had suffered with dysentery died, and a burial was arranged within three hours. The little body was neatly sewn up with a quantity of sand that would facilitate its fall downwards into the deep, and Captain Wales said funeral prayers over it before it was sent to its watery grave. It was a very sad occasion with the bereaved parents weeping, the mother particularly grieved and questioning herself as to whether she could have done anything to prevent the death. Dr Grant did his best to reassure her that she had not been at fault, and her husband led her back to their quarters in the steerage where several of her fellow passengers, mothers themselves, offered comfort.

At breakfast Laure noticed that Douglas looked more serious than usual and wondered why that was, but nothing was said. Douglas did not wish to mention such a sad happening because, having noticed Laure's affection towards the children she had seen on the ship, he knew that she would be deeply affected by the child's death. So Laure and her fellow passengers partook of breakfast in complete oblivion of this occurrence.

John Browning shows his family likenesses

When Laure, the Sedgewicks, the Walters and Henry Manning were gathered on the poop deck John Browning brought out the daguerreotypes of his parents and sister. He also showed them a portrait of his younger brother, painted on porcelain. The ladies were full of admiration at the beauty of this young boy with his large brown eyes and curling fair hair. They also commented on the sweet expression the artist had captured, his gently smiling mouth. "But," said Laure, "he looks very delicate."

John sighed and said, "My poor brother was an invalid, and I am sorry to say that he died at the age of thirteen. I decided to become a teacher because I so enjoyed instructing him in reading and writing and the other subjects that he was missing, his ill health making him unable to attend school." Everyone commented sympathetically on John's loss and told him that they could understand his choice of career.

Suddenly Henry Manning looked up and said, "There is a ship in the distance!"

The whole party went to Orient's side and saw the ship. At that distance it was not possible for them to see what flag she was flying. Turning to one of the officers Henry Manning asked him when he thought the ship would reach them. The officer replied that it would probably take until that evening at the speed he discerned it to be travelling.

"If it remains calm," asked Henry, "might it be possible for Orient to lower a boat and, if she is on her way back to England, enquire whether we could ask for our letters home to be delivered?"

He was told by the officer that the calms in the tropics were very treacherous, but if there were little or no wind the next morning it might be possible to make contact with the approaching ship. The captains would hail each other through their speaking trumpets. It would be necessary of course to make sure that Orient was not in danger if the other ship was a vagabond. This sent a shiver of apprehension through the party of cabin passengers and they were glad that Douglas Wales and his officers had firearms on board, just in case.

After all John Browning's family likenesses had been looked at, and excited discussion entered into by all as to the possibility of a nefarious vessel advancing towards Orient, the group dispersed for refreshments in the saloon. John Browning though held back slightly, and then walked along to join Douglas as he went towards the helm, telescope at the ready to view the approaching vessel.

John Browning seeks Douglas' advice

"Captain Wales," he said, "might I presume on your goodwill to ask your advice on a personal matter?"

"I should be pleased to be of assistance to you if I can," said Douglas. "In what way can I help?"

The two men moved towards the rail, Douglas waiting for John to speak. Blushing, the younger man looked out over the sea for a second or two while he formulated his request. Looking then directly at Douglas he said, "I have become enamoured of a young lady passenger, sir, and I am at a loss as to how to proceed."

"Since Mademoiselle Volpéliére is the only young single lady passenger on my ship," Douglas said, "I deduce that she is the lady you refer to." John nodded.

Douglas found himself extremely disturbed by this declaration. He had of course noticed that Laure seemed to enjoy talking to John at mealtimes, and Laure had been very determined to join in one of his classes. What if she began to be impatient with Douglas' wish to delay courting her? What if being called away so often, because of his countless duties in running his ship, caused her to see so much more of John Browning that he began to usurp Douglas' place in her heart? Was Laure so fickle? She was very young. John was handsome, young and available as a shipboard companion whenever he was not teaching. He brought books of English grammar and literature to the saloon and, when the weather was inclement, he and Laure studied these together. Douglas, feeling that he was being too slow to respond to John, said quickly, "Why do you find it difficult to proceed, Mr Browning?"

John's answer so mirrored Douglas' own thoughts about courtship on board a sailing vessel on the high seas that he almost laughed out loud. John bewailed the fact that he could not buy a bouquet of flowers to give to Laure, nor could he purchase any small gift to give to her – sweetmeats, perhaps, that could be enjoyed by her mother also.

"You could write her a poem," he told John. "If you cannot compose one yourself, surely you have one in a book which would be appropriate and could be copied."

"That is an excellent idea, Captain. I am indebted to you," the younger man said. He went off happily towards the saloon, and Douglas made his way to the helm, feeling that he had been too generous with his advice. He comforted himself with the thought that from what he had observed of Laure's character she did not seem the sort of young woman to be dazzled by a new younger suitor. He only hoped he was right.

That night in his cabin between watches Douglas pondered on John Browning's words earlier in the day. Laure's action in rushing to his side after the mutiny was proof enough of her feelings of love for him, surely. He must try to set aside these misgivings and stop torturing himself. However it now seemed imperative that he seek an interview with Suzanne Volpélière and tell her of his love for her daughter, and his wish to marry her. An engagement or an understanding between Douglas and Laure would make it impossible for another man to begin to court her. A meeting with her mother must be arranged and the invitation sent as soon as possible.

The prisoners petition Douglas Wales

He then turned to a matter in hand relating to the group of prisoners who had been confined after the mutiny. A week had now passed since the mutiny, and that afternoon Douglas had received a petition from these prisoners in which they promised good conduct and prayed for liberation. On reviewing his report of the appalling behaviour of the prisoners towards him, Douglas' immediate impulse was to refuse the petition and hand them over on arrival to the authorities in Port Phillip as had been his initial reaction on the day of the mutiny. If he took this course of action, the men would be imprisoned for a very long time, and on their release no self-respecting master of a ship would employ them as crew with such a history. They might never succeed in returning to their country of origin.

There was also the fact that taking on new crew members to replace these men might not be an easy task. Seamen wishing to leave the ship they had arrived in and transfer to another ship might be disgruntled with their previous master and be troublemakers. At least Douglas knew what he was up against with the men who were petitioning him. If he acted compassionately and gave them a second chance, the miscreants were likely to be grateful to him and might therefore go about their duties without causing further trouble.

Douglas looked at the portrait of his mother that hung above the desk in his cabin. Beside it was a small store of books she had given him when he first began to sail the oceans of the world, the poetry of Milton and Shakespeare, his small Bible and the Book of Common Prayer amongst them. His mother had suffered. Only two of her five sons were now alive, Douglas and his brother William, a clergyman in Northampton. Three sons had lost their lives, one having been swept overboard and drowned when he was a young entrant to the East India Company. Douglas' father, John, died at the early age of forty four when working in India and his mother, Maria Catherine, at the time of her husband's death, had been left widowed with five young sons. Her religion sustained Maria Catherine, and Douglas had been greatly influenced by her compassion towards all she met and her sense of fairness. He decided to let the prisoners return to work and he called in the officer of the watch and gave the order to take the prisoners out of confinement, but Douglas added: "Keep a constant eye upon them for the rest of the journey."

The mutinous sailors were thankful to be released and grateful to their captain for deciding to take that course rather than the more punitive one that would result in imprisonment in Australia.

The other ship

The next morning the weather was fine. The previous long heaving swell of the ocean had mainly subsided and the wind had gradually lessened. The ship they had all observed the previous day was now much closer to Orient and was seen to be flying the Red Ensign and, because of the calmness of the sea, two of the officers and a few passengers proceeded to row towards her in the quarter boat. As they approached the other ship it was seen that her name was Caroline. When they boarded her they found that she was on her way from Sydney, laden with a cargo of wool and oil for London. Caroline's voyage from Sydney had taken three months so far, a much longer journey than had been expected. They were out of flour, tea and sugar, and asked if Orient could supply these for their five cabin passengers. In return it was agreed that Caroline would take home letters written by passengers in Orient. Some of these had started writing the evening before, just in case this would happen. Caroline's captain was invited by Douglas to dine with him and his passengers that evening, and when the Caroline's Captain arrived the two sailors enjoyed some nautical conversation after which all the passengers joined them.

A small shark had been caught that morning. It was about four feet long and those who sampled it when cooked found it delicious. Caroline's captain brought with him a basket of oranges, some chocolate and a case of claret. A boat was sent to his ship from Orient with two barrels of flour, a large bag of sugar and a dozen pounds of tea.

Having someone new at the dinner table, especially one who had seen Australia, was fascinating to all Orient's cabin passengers. They were able to ask questions about life in the colony. Captain Gerald, captain of the ship Caroline, told them that there were good shops with medicines, groceries, haberdashery and ironmongery to be found when going on land in Melbourne. Indeed each shop seemed to be quite an emporium. He continued that there were many beautiful flowering shrubs, the wild geranium among them, and that although there were not many birds, those there were had a sweet song. Every little matter connected with the shore was of great importance to Orient's passengers, and Laure decided that she would lose no time in passing on this information to the Harris family.

The cost of a piece of land had risen extraordinarily due to the fact that a lot of it had been bought up by Sydney speculators who doled it out at a far greater price than would have been the case a few months previously. This land was being divided up into small pieces and sold at auction for upwards of £10,000. Twenty five shillings per foot was asked as a rental upon the supposed value of the land. Those newcomers to Melbourne who had no capital available to invest in land had to arrange such a lease, and any building they erected on this piece of land would become the property of the owner of the land to whom they paid rent.
"I have brought a tent," James Walters told Captain Gerald. "What sort of protection will it give?"

"There can be weeks of storm, of thunder and lightning and dense downpours of rain," he replied. "The wind can upset a tent and rain can come through the top of it. You would be better off to rent small rooms until such time as you are employed and can put up a wooden house." James and Agnes looked worriedly at each other and wondered how soon James could find employment.

"Do you have any information as to the sort of wages that are paid?" James asked.

"Labourers are paid between 7 and 10 shillings a day," the Captain told him. "Brickmakers, bricklayers, carpenters, joiners, smiths, shoemakers and tailors 12 to 16 shillings; a man and wife as house servants would be paid £30 to £50 a year and would be fed; house servants £15 to £25, clerks from £100 to £300 a year."

"And what could lodgings cost?" asked Agnes.

"Respectable board and lodging cannot be obtained under £2.2 shillings per week," was the answer.

Anne Sedgewick then asked, "What is the price of foodstuffs, Captain Gerald?"

"I am told that fish is 6 pence or 8 pence per lb, cabbages 6 pence to 1 shilling each, eggs 6 pence, fresh butter 2 shillings 6 pence to 3 shillings per lb, salt 2 shillings to 2 shillings 8 pence." He went on, looking in a notebook he had taken from his pocket: "Carrots 3 pence, onions 2 pence per lb, apples and plums 2 pence each, milk 6 pence."

"You have taken a great deal of trouble to note all these prices down," said Anne, and the other ladies all expressed their consternation as to the exorbitant prices Captain Gerald had quoted.

"My wife asked me to find all this out," said the captain; "she wished to know so that she could pass the information on to people in her church. Some of the ladies in the congregation visit the poor, and imparting knowledge such as this might be helpful to those amongst them who are contemplating emigration."

When the Caroline's captain returned to his ship he carried with him a bag of letters for England from many of the passengers, both paying and assisted emigrants.

"I suppose a kitchen garden would be one of the first things to cultivate," said Peter Sedgewick, as the group in the saloon settled down to coffee and liqueurs, "once one had been able to lease a small piece of land."

The two couples, Sedgewicks and Walters, talked quietly amongst themselves after hearing all the information Captain Gerald had imparted. It was obviously going to be imperative that the young husbands find employment as soon as possible on arrival in Melbourne. Agnes Walters said to James, "I am not at all happy about living in a tent at first. I know it was a good idea of yours to buy one in England, but being drenched, or having the tent blown away, that would be dreadful for a newborn child, to say nothing of its parents too!"

"We must think again," James replied. "A clerking job as soon as I can and perhaps you and our infant, when it is born, can be in lodgings while I sleep in the tent. That might cost less than our needing a larger room for both you and me."

"I should hate for us to be apart!" Agnes cried. "And more so now that my time is drawing nearer." James was glad that he had brought an excellent reference from his previous employer in England and also that he was strong and healthy.

"I can give you the name of a respectable lodging house and also the name of a merchant in Melbourne who may well need, or know of another who needs, an efficient clerk," said Douglas, who had caught some of the young people's conversation.

"That would be capital, sir," said James. "Might you also know of a physician? I should like to know that Agnes is having the right care for her confinement."

"I do not myself," replied Douglas, "but Dr Grant may well do so." The surgeon superintendent was not amongst the party that evening. He had elected to rest in his cabin after being occupied in the men's sick bay all day. He had operated on a member of crew who had broken his kneecap by slipping and falling on a spar when there was a spurt of bad weather during his watch the night before.

John Browning speaks to Laure

Listening to the conversation about life in the new colony Laure felt envious of those passengers who were going on in Orient, having left her and her mother behind in Mauritius. Douglas would sail off out of her life once she disembarked at Port Louis. Would that she could stay on the ship with Douglas! Indeed she longed to travel with him wherever he went. The thought of being separated from him filled her with sadness. John Browning noticed that she was suddenly very quiet and with an unhappy look that was not her usual expression at all.

"You seem preoccupied, Mademoiselle Laure," he said. "Have Captain Gerald's words about life in Australia caused you to be anxious for your shipboard friends and their future in the colony?"

"Yes, you could say so," replied Laure. By now she was able to understand what was being said and to express her thoughts far better in English, and she enjoyed practising her newly found skill - after all it could only bring her closer to Douglas Wales. She still found the English pronunciation of his Christian name difficult since in French it would be pronounced "Doogla". Secretly in her bunk at night Laure would whisper the name with both pronunciations when she knew by her snores that Suzanne was asleep.

"I should like to help to raise your spirits," John told her. "Are you fond of poetry?" When Laure nodded, John said, "I have found some very beautiful verses by Lord Alfred Tennyson."

"What is the subject of them?" asked Laure.

"They describe the poet's feelings of affection for a young lady of his acquaintance. It would make me very happy should do me the honour of reading them."

"Why do you want me to read them, John?" asked Laure "Do you have such a young lady in mind yourself? Are your affections engaged?" She showed no enthusiasm at all.

The young man reddened with embarrassment. Laure's reply, spoken so calmly and in a totally neutral manner, made it obvious to him that she did not entertain the possibility that she might be the object of his affection. If she had realized that she was, John felt she might have answered in a less detached way. Because of this he felt unsure how to proceed and he was relieved therefore when Suzanne addressed her daughter.

"When you have finished your coffee, *chérie*, please come to our cabin. I have something to show you." Suzanne then left the saloon and went to their cabin. In her hand she carried a letter she had been handed a little earlier by one of the stewards. It was from Douglas Wales, asking that she and Laure take tea with him at 6 o'clock the following day in the Great Cabin.

When Laure heard about Douglas' invitation, her heart leaped and she was filled with hope. Suzanne's reaction however was more guarded, so taking her cue from this Laure simply thanked her mother for showing her the invitation and agreed with her that it was kind of Douglas to think of inviting them. The young woman found it difficult to get off to sleep that night due to her excitement in anticipation of what she felt sure would bring her great happiness.

The day of the meeting between Douglas, Suzanne and Laure

Having woken very early on the day of the meeting with Douglas, Laure went on deck and was in time to see the sun rising out of the tropical sea. She was awed by the sight. The sun came up like an immense globe of fire surrounded by beautifully variegated clouds of every hue and form. Laure raised her face up and said aloud, "Dear Lord God, what a wonderful world you have created." The sun would not rise thus in the tropics again, as the ship would pass out of the Tropic of Capricorn during the day. The warmth they had experienced until then would give way to a colder temperature later that day.

After admiring the colours of sky and sea Laure made her way to the saloon for breakfast. John Browning and Henry Manning were the only other passengers as yet. John Browning felt embarrassment as well as disappointment when he saw Laure. He hoped that she had not realized his intention to court her. If she had realized it, then he needed to overcome these unwelcome feelings and behave as a gentleman should under the same circumstances. If she had not realized that he wished to court her then all was well and he had not lost face. The day before, after her reaction to his mention of a poem, he had given much thought to the matter. He remembered Captain Wales' eagerness to dance with Laure and her pleasure at being partnered by the captain. He recalled the two of them sitting close together on the deck a week or two before and how Laure had smiled up at Douglas.

Laure had hung on to every word Douglas Wales had spoken when he described the journey through the Grand Barrier Reef and his brave rescue of the captain, passengers and crew of a stricken ship. He remembered how she had slipped away when the mutiny on board was over, and the expression on her face. Thinking back he admitted to himself that he had been so taken up with his feelings for the young French woman that he had missed the clues that would have prevented him from attempting to woo Laure. Now it was obvious to him that the captain was the man she held above all other.

As the Sedgewicks and the Walters joined them for breakfast, it was good, John thought, that the conversation became general. He could detect no obvious sign that Laure had any inkling of his romantic attachment to her. She asked him about the class he was teaching that morning and discussed a copy of 'Lamb's Tales from Shakespeare' that he had lent her after the lesson she attended. She remained the same friendly person he had known, and he was relieved although saddened. "Let the better man win," he told himself.

In another part of Orient the male cabin passengers had the opportunity to try their hand at shooting. Their targets were the birds which flew above and around the ship. It was a favourite if somewhat cruel and unnecessary pastime, but it did assist in alleviating some of the boredom that a long voyage such as this one could engender. The Albatross, Black Petrel, Blue Petrel and Stormy Petrel abounded and also some very large gulls, but shooting them was, some of the ladies felt, a thoroughly useless occupation as they were not good for eating and would rot before they could be sent to a taxidermist. The women sighed and shook their heads but told each other that anything that kept their menfolk occupied was to be encouraged.

At the appointed time the two women approached the captain's cabin and, on being ushered in by the officer on duty at the door, they found themselves in the large and well-furnished room, the tall windows of which let in a great deal of light. On the floor was a dark blue carpet, and placed round a well-polished and large table were comfortable looking high-backed chairs. This was the Great Cabin where the ship's captain entertained influential guests when in ports all over the world. The captain dined with his officers there when he did not join his cabin passengers in the saloon. It was his private domain, and nobody was allowed to enter it without his invitation. A smaller sleeping cabin was situated off the Great Cabin.

While waiting for his guests to arrive Douglas had taken up a book of poetry entitled 'The Poetical Works of John Milton', which his mother had given him. An inscription she had written on its frontispiece read:

Douglas Wales

The gift of his affectionate mother, November 1825 as a part of a small stock of books for his perusal during his voyages, and likewise to remind him whenever he looks into it of the happy, happy times he has left to venture on the wide and trackless oceans.

Reading a page or two calmed Douglas as he prepared to ask the question that he felt to be the most important of his life, because the answer to it would lead either to great happiness on the one hand or bitter disappointment on the other. Laure's mother might well irrevocably refuse to give her consent. Douglas had composed and memorized a sentence in French in which he intended to address Laure's mother and he practised it as he waited.

When all three were seated, and the ladies had been offered refreshment of wine and biscuits set out on a china plate, the conversation started mildly. The subjects of it were the weather, the length of time left before the ship docked at Port Louis, how enjoyable the dance had been, and so on.

Suzanne was still wondering why they had been summoned by Douglas. She did not feel that a request for Laure's hand in marriage could come so soon in the acquaintance of the two. It would seem premature. Therefore Suzanne was slightly anxious as she looked at Douglas enquiringly.

After about ten minutes spent in this desultory way Douglas, who had found himself becoming increasingly nervous, turned to Suzanne and, in a rather louder tone of voice than he had intended, started to speak.

"*Madame* …" he began and then to his horror he faltered, struggling to remember the French words he had previously decided to use.

"*Oui, Capitaine?*" enquired Suzanne, very surprised to see this usually confident man seemingly at a loss for words. Why, Captain Wales had become quite red in the face!

Douglas took a deep breath and blurted out: "*Madame Volpélière, je veux Laure.*" Then he sat back in his chair, a mixture of hope and fear in his expression, and waited for a reply from Laure's mother. Laure, who had had no difficulty at all in understanding Douglas' meaning, was smiling. When Suzanne turned to her, Laure was amazed to see that her mother looked very upset by Douglas' words. She whispered something to Laure in French. Before Laure could reply, Suzanne faced Douglas again and said firmly in her native tongue, "I cannot give you any more gold, Captain Wales."

Douglas was completely taken aback at this and looked blankly at Suzanne. Divining at once the confusion between her own name and the French for 'gold', *l'or*, Laure could barely restrain her laughter. Turning to Suzanne with a smile she said in their own language, "*Maman*, Captain Wales doesn't want more gold. He is saying that he wants me!" Then she said to Douglas,

"Captain Wales, my mother misunderstood you; she thought you were asking for more money for our passage."

Douglas was horrified. "*Mademoiselle*, that is the last thing I want. I was at a loss to find the right words in French. Please tell your mother that I am requesting your hand in marriage." This was said in English and Laure replied in that language.

"I myself accept your proposal, Captain Wales, with the utmost pleasure." Douglas beamed, delighted. Turning to Suzanne and in the best French he could muster, he apologized that he had expressed himself so badly, and repeated that his fervent wish was that he could become engaged to Laure and marry her eventually.

Suzanne, having feared a financial dilemma, was now faced with one of a different kind. In French, but with Laure translating, she said to Douglas, "Captain, my daughter is young, but I can see that she holds you in great affection and respect."

Douglas inclined his head gratefully.

"However, Captain Wales," Suzanne continued, "we are of the Roman Catholic religion. We would need her father's permission to marry before the age of twenty one, and I very much fear that he would not grant it unless you took our religion. For generations the Volpélières have been Catholic."

Laure interpreted her mother's words and both she and Douglas looked worriedly at each other.

"To change my religion and become Roman Catholic would be well-nigh impossible for me, *Madame*," were Douglas' words that Laure translated for Suzanne. "My widowed mother is a staunch upholder of the Anglican religion, and she would be very distressed if I thought of changing to another. My mother has suffered greatly in her life and at her age now I could not contemplate causing her distress."

To his consternation he saw that Laure's face, so recently happy and joyous, had become sad, and that tears were in her eyes as she relayed Douglas' words to Suzanne.

"Permit me, *Madame*," he said to Suzanne, and then he reached out his right hand and took Laure's hand in his. At Douglas' touch Laure recovered her composure. She spoke in English to Douglas: "Sad as I would be to entirely lose any love my father still has for me, I intend to do all I must do to become your wife. After all, I would be making a new life for myself, far away from France and from my father and his relations, and to be prevented for any reason from marrying the man I love would be infinitely worse. I shall take your religion, if necessary." Laure repeated her declaration to Suzanne in French.

Douglas, filled with admiration for her determination and her love, lifted up her hand to his lips and kissed it.

"I adore your daughter, *Madame*," he said and found that suddenly he had no difficulty with the French language, even if his accent left much to be desired. "I would do everything in my power to bring her nothing but happiness."

"Please tell Captain Wales that I believe what he says," Suzanne told Laure. She went on: "I have learned to respect his courage and generosity of spirit towards his crew and to the assisted emigrant passengers under his care." Shaking her head then she went on: "It would sadden me to see my child give up her religion for another but I promise to give the matter of an engagement much thought."

When Laure had interpreted all her mother had said, Douglas spoke gently and courteously to Suzanne: "But of course, *Madame*. You must take as much time as you need. No decision can be made lightly in such an important matter as this."

"*Maman*," said Laure, when she had imparted this to Suzanne, "we no longer belong in France. The future is now a completely different one to that which we might have envisaged had we remained in Paris." Suzanne agreed and, as the two ladies left his cabin, Douglas sent up a prayer to his Maker that a satisfactory solution for them all would be reached. Then he turned his attention once more to the task of captaining Orient.

Laure knew better than to question her mother immediately as to what her decision about an engagement between Douglas and Laure would be. She knew that her mother would be pondering it deeply and would be less likely to be in favour of such a match if she felt that Laure was urging her to make her decision too hastily.

Suzanne was more than a little worried about the matter if the truth be told. To discard Roman Catholicism was a dreadful thing to do, she thought, remembering the words of priests who had told her when she was a child that those who were not Catholics would be sent to Hell and be burned for all eternity. Growing up had left her less sure of the veracity of these dire warnings, but deep down there still remained the feeling of it being wrong to leave the Church. Suzanne however knew that there had been important changes regarding the Catholic Faith in France in the latter part of the eighteenth century.

Religion in France after the Revolution, that began in 1789 and did not end until the late 1790s, had at first, along with the abolition of feudal rights, meant that titles were to be no more and men free to worship God in whatever way they pleased. What then followed was the reform of the legal system and reform of the clergy. In 1790 a further development ensued in that the religious orders were suppressed. Then a decree was passed giving all the church lands and property to the nation, every priest had to take an oath to serve the Civil Constitution of the Clergy, now part of the state, and the Pope's authority was no more. Even in Mauritius, when Napoleon Bonaparte ruled France, children were no longer given the names of saints, but the edict was that they were given the names of plants and herbs. Until there was once more a king in France, Suzanne was known as '*Sauge*' (sage), 'Suzanne' being a derivative of 'Saint Anne'.

How would Henri Volpélière react when he received the news of his daughter's defection to the Protestant faith? Not that he had obeyed the tenets of any form of Christianity himself so rigidly. The various amours he had had while still being married to Suzanne were proof of that. Suzanne found that her thoughts and feelings were in turmoil, making it impossible for her to decide what her answer to Douglas Wales would be. She felt buffeted in first one direction and then another in her mind. She tried to imagine a scenario in which Henri might be less against such a marriage for his daughter, but each time she came to the point of Henri giving his blessing to the couple, reality set in, and she knew she was indulging in wishful thinking. As to what her own thoughts were in the matter, again she became confused and unable to be firmly convinced either way. Listing pros and cons only made things worse.

Two lone women, with very little money, needing to be dependent on relations in Mauritius would be much more secure if Laure eventually was married to Douglas – a man of means with a fine future ahead of him owning a trading vessel such as Orient. Did she really need to consult Henri at all? He would probably be very angry if a marriage went ahead without his knowledge. Suzanne found it difficult to sleep that night and in the morning, as it was fine, she went up on the deck to enjoy the fresh air. She decided to give herself a rest from worrying thoughts for now.

OCEAN ADVENTURE 1840

Laure introduces Jane Harris to Agnes Walters

The same morning Laure tapped on the cabin door of James and Agnes Walters. When Agnes opened it, Laure said, "Would you care to meet the wife of the man who wrote to Captain Wales, seeking to be introduced to an employer in Australia?"

"Yes indeed," replied Agnes. "Being a mother herself, she would seem to be an ideal person to assist me. I would find it most reassuring to have her advice."

"It is washing day today," said Laure. "Let us go to the main deck to see if she is putting some wet clothes out to dry."

The two young women found Jane Harris pegging out washed clothing onto the rigging where it cheerfully blew about in the wind. "It will be dry before you can say 'Jack Robinson,'" Jane said to Agnes. The three women sat together on the deck and Laure made the introduction. Agnes was impressed by Jane's courageous determination to do all she could to build a good life for her family. Her genuine wish to serve was clearly apparent in her choice of words and in her manner.

"I would do my very best, Mrs Walters," she said, "to help you to have confidence regarding the birth of your child. I frequently assisted my mother, who attended at many births in our village, being called in for her experience as a midwife. Several generations of children were brought into the world by her."

"Such expertise would be most welcome," said Agnes. "It would also be of benefit for me to be able to learn from you all that is necessary in care of the newborn infant. I had no younger brothers or sisters, and very few of my friends are married yet. Experience of such things is lacking in my case."

"Nature has a way of leading a new mother in the right direction," said Jane with a smile.

"You realize that until my husband has found employment we could only offer to share accommodation and food with you and your family?" Agnes asked her.

"Yes indeed," replied Jane. "I know George too will do everything in his power to find employment, and if our little family is more quickly successful in that, why, we would be able to pay at least for our food." Agnes was touched by Jane's sincerity. She felt she had truly found a friend in Jane.

Laure was delighted with the success of the meeting between Agnes and Jane. She looked forward to telling Douglas about it and hurried to the quarterdeck in the hopes of finding him there, leaving Jane and Agnes deep in conversation. She was disappointed when she did not see Douglas near the helm and somewhat tentatively moved to the poop deck towards her mother, who was sitting quietly reading. As Laure drew up a chair beside her mother, Suzanne asked her, "What is it about Captain Wales that has determined you to become his wife, my child? It seems to me that he is unsuitable in all but one way."

"What is that one way, *Maman*?" Laure said.

"Only that he is a man of some means. Otherwise he is much older than you are, he is not Roman Catholic, trading is his occupation, he leads a life on the high seas with no settled home in any country and his knowledge of the French language and the way of life of people such as ourselves leaves much to be desired," Suzanne replied.

"You are forgetting entirely his compassion, courage and sense of fairness," Laure replied, and she went on: "Do you not also think, *Maman*, that he is a fine figure of a man, that his eyes are expressive, that he is a courteous gentleman and looks most dashing in his uniform?"

"I agree with all that," Suzanne replied, "but his appearance is really not important in the scheme of things."

"Oh but, *Maman*, it is very important indeed to me!" said Laure. "Think what beautiful children we might have, grandchildren who would love their severe grandmother and help her to forget the bad things of the past. For me, this brave man is quite irresistible and I would go to the ends of the earth to become his wife. Should I be prevented from attaining my heart's desire, *Maman*, I will droop and pine and you will see me fade away before you."

Suzanne looked at her daughter's round face, its plump rosy cheeks and her bright eyes. She certainly looked determined to say the least, and most unlikely to become wraithlike.

"I simply do not know what to do," Suzanne said. "It will take many months before a letter reaches your father. You must realize that I alone cannot give my consent."

"But could we not be allowed to become engaged?" asked Laure. "Then we would know that there was hope of our having a future together, and we would be able to speak together and learn more about each other without the presence of a chaperone."

"I promise I will consider this," Suzanne said. "After all, in the circumstances we find ourselves now - far from land, passengers in a sailing ship that we share with many others and even with animals - ordinary social rules might be set aside perhaps."

Laure flung her arms around her mother and kissed her. "When I marry, you shall be an important part of our family life, *Maman*," she told Suzanne. "Think what a blessing it will be for me to have your guidance in my new life. But of course I shall sail with my husband at first. We will however make sure that you have a good home."

"How do you know Captain Douglas will agree to this?" asked Suzanne. "Mothers in law are not always greatly liked by husbands!"

"I believe he will wish to do what makes me happy," her daughter replied with conviction.

Suzanne's thoughts after this conversation continued to make her anxious. On the one hand, to see her daughter happily settled and married to the man she loved, anything but the poor relation she, and Suzanne, would be on arrival in Mauritius, was a tempting prospect. On the other, the act of completely overthrowing the traces of religion and convention, and the risk of being permanently cast aside by the Volpélières, Suzanne found very worrying. With regard to religion, Suzanne told herself that it was not as if Laure, in taking Douglas' religion, would deny God. She would not become an atheist. Indeed religion, albeit of a different persuasion, would be an important part in the life of Laure and Douglas.

Suzanne writes to Douglas

Laure's remark about making Suzanne a part of her future family if she married Douglas was extremely pleasing to Suzanne. It gave her hope that she might continue to be a person in her own right, a helpful addition to her daughter's life. A good marriage for her daughter was surely a desirable achievement for any mother, especially when the mother was unable to provide her daughter with a dowry. The scales were beginning to weigh in Douglas' favour by the time Suzanne joined the assembled company for the midday meal.

It was an enjoyable gathering at the table that day. Douglas and Laure were consumed with happiness because they knew they loved each other and that they would be able to marry, even if they had to wait until Laure reached her majority.

James and Agnes Walters were content to have made an arrangement with Jane and George Harris once they landed in Melbourne. Douglas Wales had given Peter Sedgewick an introductory letter to a merchant of his acquaintance who might need an accountant. John Browning knew that there were prospects for him in Australia. He was enduring his disappointment regarding his feelings for Laure well, even if he was embarrassed that Douglas knew of them. He had however observed that there was no difference now in the way Douglas spoke to or looked at him. Everything seemed just the same as though his declaration had never taken place.

Henry Manning was discussing the Protestant religion with Suzanne. She asked him many questions about the differences between it and Roman Catholicism. What struck her most during this conversation were the many similarities between the two, and this pleased her.

Douglas had placed Laure on his left at the table, with Suzanne opposite her. He was glad that Suzanne was absorbed in her discussion with Henry Manning as it allowed him to concentrate fully on Laure.

"It is difficult to be patient in waiting for your mother's decision on our future," he said quietly.

"Indeed it is!" Laure agreed. "But I have every hope that eventually she will allow us to become engaged at least. I know she wishes me to be happy and that I could not be so without you at my side."

"We must be patient and hopeful," Douglas replied.

"I have told my mother that we will regard her as part of our family when we marry," said Laure. She continued: "I also told her that I was sure you would agree to this because you will wish to make me happy, and I could not be truly happy knowing that my poor mother is cast aside and left to be a poor relation of the Bérichon or Chipault families in Mauritius."

Slightly surprised by this Douglas waited a second or two before answering, and Laure had a brief moment of anxiety. Douglas however said, "Naturally your mother will be cared for by us both, my dear. She will be accorded every respect by me."

"I suppose I must wait until I am twenty one," said Laure. "At that age I can marry without permission from my father. I am sorry that this is necessary, but I am afraid he will not give his consent. He is still influenced by his family and I know they will put forward a good case against my change of religion."

When later on that day in their cabin Laure told Suzanne what Douglas had said, Suzanne smiled at her daughter: "He is a good man, *chérie*. We are both lucky to have met him and I must tell you that my discussions with

Mr Manning this midday have helped me to make a decision. I shall allow an engagement between you and Douglas Wales."

Laure leaped from her chair and, clasping her mother in a tight embrace, rained kisses on her face. Finally Suzanne protested that her cap, her hair and her garments were becoming disordered, and Laure withdrew. Still clasping Suzanne by the hand she said, "Must I wait until tomorrow to tell him?"

"I must write to him to make it official," her mother replied. She sat down at the table to write, and shortly afterwards sent a steward with the letter to Douglas' cabin.

Douglas receives Suzanne's letter

Douglas, having received the letter in its closed envelope, stood for at least a minute with it unopened in his hand. What if Laure was wrong in being hopeful about her mother's decision? What would he do if she refused to give permission even to an engagement? Might such a refusal mean that Douglas would need to travel to France to petition Henri Volpélière for his daughter's hand in marriage? Would he be forced to become Roman Catholic in spite of the grief he would cause his mother? Douglas never for one moment considered the possibility that he would not marry Laure. That was unthinkable. His thoughts whirled about in his mind, causing him to feel quite dizzy and to pull a chair towards him and sit heavily down on it. Only then, after taking a deep breath to calm himself, did he reach for a paper opener and neatly slit the top of the envelope. Taking the thin piece of paper from it he realized that of course it was written in French. The handwriting was extremely spidery and he would need to use a magnifying glass and a French/English dictionary to read Suzanne's missive.

Suzanne wrote that, because it was impossible to obtain the permission of her husband, being far from land and very far from France, and because she felt that the present circumstances were so extreme in their difference to those that would have constituted a normal courtship, she had decided to exercise her right as a parent to permit Captain Wales and her beloved daughter, Laure, to become betrothed. As to the future there remained matters to be considered before a marriage could take place, the main consideration, after that of religion, being that her daughter at eighteen was three years from her majority.

Douglas of course was delighted and went about his duties on board with a light heart, looking forward with happy anticipation to seeing Laure at dinner that evening.

Laure in the meantime having wheedled her mother's answer from Suzanne before the despatch of the letter to Douglas, spent the remaining hours before dinner deciding which of her few dresses would be the most appropriate to wear in celebration of the occasion.

Laure and Douglas are affianced

At the end of dinner that evening Douglas turned to Suzanne and said, "With your permission, *Madame*, I should like to announce my betrothal to your daughter." Suzanne agreed, and Douglas rose to his feet. "Ladies and gentleman," he said when conversation had ceased and all eyes were on him, "I have an announcement to make to you of the happiest kind." He then turned to Laure, who was regarding him with shining eyes. "Mademoiselle Laure has consented to become my fiancée. Madame Volpélière, her mother, has given us her permission and we hope to be married as soon as it becomes possible."

There were delighted cries of congratulation from all those at the table. The young married women left their chairs and came to kiss Laure. The officers present and Henry Manning offered their hands to shake Douglas', and glasses were raised in honour of the happy couple. Laure came to stand beside Douglas and slipped her hand into his. She looked, thought Douglas, at her most beautiful that evening in the colour that best suited her. She had chosen the apricot coloured silk dress she had worn at the dance on board. He bent towards her and said quietly, "My dearest, I wish I had a beautiful ring to give you, but all I have with me is my signet ring." He smiled and added: "I did not expect to become engaged to be married on this journey! I am afraid it will be too big for your finger, but perhaps you have the means to wear it around your neck on a ribbon or a gold chain?" Douglas took the heavy gold ring from the little finger of his right hand and handed it to Laure.

Laure, after lifting it to her lips and kissing it, said, "I have just the thing – it shall be threaded onto my jet necklace. I shall wear it with pride." Bending her head down she indicated that Douglas should unclasp the necklace and, when he had done so, and the signet ring was in place, he fastened the clasp of the necklace once more. The happy couple then exchanged their first kiss and their companions all clapped.

John Browning then proposed a toast to the gallant Captain Wales and Mademoiselle Laure, and felt pleased that he was able to be happy for the couple even though his own feelings for Laure had not been returned by her.

When dinner was over, Douglas told those at the table that when Orient arrived at the Cape of Good Hope he intended to put in at Cape Town for fresh water, vegetables and other commodities. The passengers were overjoyed to hear that they would be able to go ashore since the ship would remain there for two days and a night before continuing her journey. Douglas then left them and went to his quarters accompanied by several of his officers.

When they had left, Suzanne announced that she was going to rest in her cabin, and the two young married women, Agnes and Anne, began excitedly to converse with Laure regarding her engagement.

"I was not at all surprised!" exclaimed Agnes.
"Neither was I!" Anne said. "It was clear that Captain Douglas' affections were engaged almost from the

beginning of this journey. How soon did you realize this?"

Laure blushed slightly as she replied: "I *thought* I saw a liking of me when our friends in London introduced my mother and me to Captain Wales. I could not be sure of course, and I needed time to observe him and to come to terms with my own sentiments before I came to the realization that we loved each other. But, even when I knew and he knew that we were meant for each other, there seemed to be unsurmountable obstacles to our marrying."

"The main one," said Agnes with a teasing smile, "being *Madame*, your mother, perhaps?"

"Oh, poor *Maman*!" said Laure and she told her two friends about her mother's misunderstanding of Douglas' proposal. Anne and Agnes were amused but in a kindly way. They knew how difficult the language barrier had been for the French woman surrounded as she had been by English men and women.

When Laure told them of Suzanne's discussion with Henry Manning, and her realisation that becoming a Protestant was not such a heinous crime given the changes in Roman Catholicism in France since the Revolution and the similarities in both religions, they became serious and confessed to admiration for Suzanne for her open-mindedness.

"What my father will say remains to be seen," Laure went on. "I think he will not cut me out of his life completely. He was very unhappy to see me go and, if it had been possible, he would have preferred me to stay in Paris with him and for my mother to go back to Mauritius alone. This was simply not at all *comme-il-faut* - socially acceptable."

Laure's eyes suddenly widened. "Heavens!" she said. "To think that I might have not come on this voyage, and so never met Douglas!"

Arrival in Cape Town

There was stormy weather around the Cape of Good Hope, but fortunately it was not as bad as the storm Orient's passengers had endured earlier in the voyage. To be sure, it was difficult to keep the chairs in the saloon from sliding about at mealtimes, and in the 'tween deck items fell off hooks and shelves, and there was discomfort amongst all passengers, cabin and steerage. However the storms were of shorter duration and it was not necessary to batten down the hatches. No one was injured and most passengers seemed to have obtained their sea legs by then.

The sight of Table Mountain amazed all those who saw it for the first time. Nine hundred feet high with a tempestuous sky above it and, to the left, a sunlit valley between the Lion's Head and the Devil's Peak - it looked awe inspiring. All on board were either rendered speechless by it or moved to cry out: *"How wonderful!" "How amazing!"* Laure and Anne Sedgwick were joined by Agnes Walters on the poop deck. They were all excited at the prospect of going ashore later on that morning. Douglas, some of the officers, Peter Sedgwick and James Walters would be accompanying them.

Faced with the welcome prospect of being able to go ashore for the first time for many weeks, the crew were extremely cheerful. They knew, as did all sailors before them, that Cape Town was considered the 'sailor's tavern', and they also looked forward to fresh meat, fruit and vegetables. The possibility of making the acquaintance of compliant females added to their enthusiasm and they set to work happily preparing to bring the ship alongside in the harbour.

The emigrant passengers in Orient were also able to gain benefit from this stop. They were divided into groups of thirty, and representatives for each group were appointed from amongst them. Those passengers who had funds gave their representative lists of items to purchase in Cape Town. Fresh fruit and vegetables were the most popular items requested, with wine or beer for the men coming second, and then sweets for the children.

Laure had gone to find Jane Harris early in the morning, and promised to purchase a piece of material suitable to make a new jacket for George. "So that he can make a good impression, Miss, if he is granted an interview for work," Jane had said.

Douglas had business to transact in Cape Town. He needed to take more fresh water on board as well as fruit and vegetables, and needed to purchase some more poultry and sheep to replace the ones whose slaughter had provided the fresh meat for those on Orient who were entitled to it. He had decided not to linger long in the South African port, feeling that it would be unfair to the emigrant passengers if some of the people on board were able to spend time enjoying dry land and civilization whilst others were not. One night was all Douglas allowed some of his crew, and all categories of Orient's passengers would sleep on the ship.

After his duties ashore Douglas intended to purchase a suitable engagement ring for Laure. Therefore he left her with Agnes and Anne in the fine shops along the main thoroughfare where they looked for materials with which to make shawls and dresses, and Laure also compared prices for worsted to make George Harris' jacket. Douglas looked for a jewellers'. He had decided that he would look on his own first of all, and then fetch Laure and ask the jeweller to show her a selection that he had chosen. In this way a discussion about the cost of the ring would not be necessary. Douglas intended to be generous, and did not want Laure to have the chance to protest at its cost.

Douglas had visited Cape Town several times and knew it well. It was easy therefore for him to accompany the young women to the most appropriate shops and, on leaving them there, make his way to a well-known jewellers'. Having explained his mission to the jeweller he was shown tray after tray of beautiful rings and eventually decided on ten rings which he asked the jeweller to put aside so that he could return with Laure, and they could make a choice together.

When they had chosen, Douglas decided, he would take Laure to the famous botanical garden where, in spite of the building in 1827 of St. George's Cathedral and of the South African College in 1838 on portions of the garden, it was still a beautiful sight.

Laure and her companions Anne and Agnes had had a most enjoyable time in the fashionable draper's shop. It had been a welcome change of scene after many weeks cooped up in Orient. They revelled in the ability to walk from counter to counter and examine every kind of material. There was also silk or cotton sewing thread of every colour and thickness, and needles and scissors. Laure found a pretty pair of scissors that she bought for Suzanne. They were small but sharp with decorated handles shaped like the heads of storks, the opening and cutting part constituting the bird's beak. For herself Laure purchased a length of blue velvet ribbon to make a belt for one of her dresses.

She was pleased with the brown worsted material she had found for George Harris' jacket. For the price the quality was excellent. Laure had added some of her own money to the cost, not much to be sure but enough to make a difference. This was to be her secret and not for the ears of the emigrant family. She had taken care not to be seen by Anne or Agnes when making the purchase.

Peter Sedgewick, James Walters and Douglas arrived together – the two young men to collect Anne and Agnes, Douglas to fetch Laure and take her down the street to the jewellers' shop. He had not told Laure of his intention to buy the ring, and she was puzzled when he led her into the shop. When she saw the trays of beautiful shining rings on the glass counter and when Douglas explained that she was to tell him which ring she liked best of all, Laure was quite overwhelmed.

"My dear," she said to Douglas, "you are too good to me. I have no idea how I can choose between them, but I must tell you that the ring I wear as a pendant is the one I shall always cherish above any other because it is the first ring you gave me." Douglas put his arm around her waist and held her close to his side as she looked at the rings. He felt that his love for her knew no bounds, and that if it had been possible he would have given her the sun, moon and stars. They both agreed on a ring at whose centre was a ruby that was encircled in gold. Douglas said he would keep it in his pocket in its velvet box and when they reached the botanical garden he would put it on Laure's finger.

It was peaceful in the garden, and the couple strolled together arm in arm, Laure wearing a wide brimmed hat to protect her from the sun which was strong. Their conversation was full of the joy of being able to plan their future together and admiring the beautiful surroundings.

By the mid-eighteenth century the garden had become famous not only for its beauty but also for the propagation and export of indigenous plants for the European market. Among these plants were pelargoniums (or geraniums and their hybrids), which were introduced in England in the mid-seventeenth century by the botanist and collector John Tradescant.

Douglas and Laure walked slowly along the central tree-lined Government Avenue with its water channels on each side, successors to the mode of irrigation at the start of the garden in its early beginnings. Laure was fascinated by an area for herbs and succulents and especially the tall common cabbage trees in the rockery, which Douglas said had medicinal properties.

"I have always been interested in the use of plants and herbs as medicines," Laure told him. She went on: "My old nurse in Paris taught me many recipes she had learned in the village she came from. Her care of me as a child included some of these draughts and ointments, and they always had the desired effect."

Douglas then led Laure towards a 200 year old tree, the Saffron Pear, planted in the seventeenth century when the Dutch East India Company started the garden, mainly to grow vegetables for their ships which traded along the eastern coast of Africa.

It was beside the ancient pear tree that Douglas took Laure's left hand in his and placed the ring on her fourth finger. They stood with their arms around each other for a short while, speechless in their happiness.

Later on Douglas and Laure joined the Walters and the Sedgwicks at a pleasant café near the waterfront where they enjoyed cool drinks and slices of cake. Peter and Anne Sedgwick had visited the Castle of Good Hope and described the gateway, built in 1682. They had been impressed by its two pilasters, entablature and pediment above, built of grey-blue stone with small yellow bricks forming the entrance: a perfect example of seventeenth century Dutch classicism. Agnes and James Walters had not ventured far because of Agnes' condition, and they were all soon joined by Henry Manning and John Browning who had hired horses and enjoyed a good gallop along Noordhoek beach.

Both young men had found this exhilarating. The clouds moving swiftly across the sky, the sea delivering its waves rhythmically onto the sands, the wind in their faces and the motion of the horses - all gave them a welcome feeling of freedom, very different from the constraint they had experienced on the ship for so many weeks. The exercise had given them a hearty appetite, and the cake soon disappeared only for more to be requested.

Laure's engagement ring was admired when she shyly showed it to Agnes and Anne. "How sad we shall be when you leave us at Mauritius!" said Agnes to Laure. "Shall we ever see each other again, do you think?"

"I shall make a point of sailing with my husband to Australia once we are married," Laure replied, "and I shall visit you. How could I not have the pleasure of seeing your child who will be born there."

"Where will you marry, sir?" Henry asked Douglas.

"In Mauritius," Douglas replied and turning to Laure he went on: "There is an Anglican church in Poudrière Street. It is a simple building without ornamentation, but it is welcoming. There is a good feeling about it. It has been used by our Army and Navy for many years, and on its walls are placed memorials to those who served in Mauritius in the past."

Douglas and Laure make plans

"When we reach Mauritius shall we go first to my aunt?" asked Laure.

"That would be the best I think," Douglas said. "I will not be able to spend any time there after you disembark as I must continue to Australia as soon as possible. Therefore I shall not be able to help you and your mother to find a house to rent until I return to Mauritius. I also need to stay in Australia for several weeks before I set off on the return journey and can anchor in Port Louis harbour."

"To think that we must be parted so soon!" Laure exclaimed.

"You are engaged to a sailor, my dearest," said Douglas. "There will, I am afraid, be many separations until I leave the sea and at present this is out of the question. I must work hard in the way I know best to make our future secure."

"But I will be able to sail with you when we are married, won't I?" Laure said anxiously. "Surely that will be possible?"

"Yes indeed, at first." Douglas replied. "The wives of ships' masters do accompany their husbands even if there is a child, but once more children come into the world it is the custom for the wives to stay ashore with them. Imagine the chaos if there were more than one or two children to be cared for on board!"

Laure laughed and replied, "One would have to have them all attached to each other by a rope, with the smallest at the back nearest to the mother." She had a mental picture of this and shuddered when she imagined a sloping deck, and children and mother losing their footing, sliding down it. She put a stop to these imaginings by gathering up her reticule, parcels and parasol in readiness to return with Douglas and the others to the waiting ship. Douglas relieved her of her parcels saying, "On my return I shall be able to spend a reasonable length of time in Mauritius and together we will find exactly the home we wish for. Then on return journeys from Australia with the ship in ballast I shall not need to make haste to return to England immediately."

Laure gives Jane Harris the material she bought

Dinner was to be on board that evening and afterwards Laure asked a woman passenger in steerage, who was taking the air on deck, if she would fetch Jane Harris up to the middle deck. Laure descended the ladder to the middle deck carrying the parcel of worsted cloth, and was standing looking over to Table Mountain when Jane came to her side. For a few moments the two young women stood quietly, entranced by the lights of Cape Town that shone out as the sky darkened. The ship was almost motionless, her sails furled, pulling slightly at her anchor the movement being more in the nature of a gentle rocking.

As Laure handed the parcel to Jane, she gently opened a small part of it so that Jane could feel the cloth. "Oh, Miss! The texture is soft but strong!" Jane exclaimed. "How can I thank you for going to this trouble for me? I have a paper pattern in my sewing box. I shall work tonight while the ship is moving so gently."

"How did you make the pattern?" asked Laure.

"When George had worn out a jacket a year ago, I unpicked it, flattened it with a hot iron and then pinned brown paper over each part of it. He has not increased in girth, so I am sure the pattern will still do very well."

"What shall you do for buttons?" Laure said.

"I have kept those from the old jacket, and I also have a store of buttons from garments worn by my grandfather." Jane replied. "I keep them in a tin box I have carried with me."

Laure was filled with admiration for Jane's resourcefulness. She wondered where the cutting of the material would take place. It would be such a delicate operation. The danger of making a false movement with the cutting scissors if the arm was jerked would have caused Laure, she thought, to avoid starting the task at all.

Jane explained that the long table where the steerage passengers sat down to eat would be available for an hour or so and she and her husband would make a clean place on it that was large enough for her to cut the worsted safely. "George will make sure that no one comes close enough to jog my arm," she said, "and I am used to making speedy cuts into materials."

"I shall look forward to seeing your husband in the jacket," Laure said. "As I am now to be married I should improve my housewifely skills. I fear though that tailoring will be beyond my capabilities."

They parted company soon after and Laure returned to the saloon where all those who had gone ashore that day were enjoying comparing notes about their experiences.

There was to be a concert that evening on deck and, as many of the emigrants were either taking part by singing or reciting and some would be playing instruments too, Jane had a clear place on the table and set to work immediately to cut out the material for George's new jacket. Her husband stayed at her side and her son watched from their bunk where he had been put to bed. He could not keep his eyes open for long though and was soon asleep and dreaming. His father had given a shore-going representative a few coins to buy fresh fruit and a toffee apple for the boy, and Georgy had enjoyed eating an orange that was deliciously sweet. The toffee apple was to be kept until the morrow.

It only took Jane Harris half an hour to complete the cutting out of the jacket, and, once she had pinned and tacked all its parts together, George was happy to have it tried on and adjusted where necessary.

"It is excellent stuff," he said to his wife. "I did not know we had enough saved to pay for material of this quality." Jane remained silent and offered up mute thanks to Miss Laure of whose generosity she had realized once the material was under her fingers. Jane knew that George's pride would have been dented if he knew that he had been given "charity", as he would have termed it. Fortunately George did not persist in questioning her. She kept him busy turning this way and that and scolding him for not keeping as still as she wished.

Some of the crew ashore at Cape Town

The three main protagonists of the mutiny on Orient, Jasper Jones, Bob Styles and Joshua Grimes - who had all three benefitted from Douglas Wales' action in setting them free from confinement in spite of their appalling behaviour towards their captain went ashore at Cape Town together. The fact that Douglas had given them permission to do so could be seen as another example of his magnanimity, but a few of the officers suspected that he was aware of the possibility that one or all of the three miscreants might not return to the ship, thus substantially reducing the chance of any further trouble among the crew!

Indeed, after seeking out a pleasant tavern, where the three men enjoyed a hearty meal of meat and fresh vegetables, and downed several tankards of excellent ale, Bob Styles lit his pipe and after a quiet time enjoying his tobacco announced that he would not return to Orient at the end of his leave.

Jasper Jones and Joshua Grimes let out low whistles, and Jasper said, "Why ever not, mate? Why jump ship where its captain is so fair?"

"I'm of the opinion," replied Bob, "that I can make a better life for myself here in South Africa. As a seaman, always taking orders from those who think they are my 'betters' angers me and fires rebellion in my breast. I fear I should always be getting myself into trouble of one sort or another shipboard."

"But how will you earn your keep?" asked Joshua. "We have all been accustomed from such an early age to be part of a ship's crew, to get our victuals done for us, and to enjoy the companionship of many."

"This place has much to offer a man," replied Bob. "I am strong and experienced. There are many ships that call in here that might need hands in harbour, or for short journeys up the east coast of Africa. I'd settle down, perhaps get me a wife, till the ground, keep a pig or two. I have saved enough to make a start."

His shipmates looked intrigued but puzzled. "Think you 'tis fair to Captain Wales," asked Joshua, "after he has been good to us all and given us a second chance? Do you not feel the need to repay him by at least working to sail the ship to Australia?"

Bob shook his head. "Nay lads, I don't. Ship will get to Australia very well without me, and I will be spared having to take orders from those younger than myself. Why, on one voyage I worked, captain was but twenty two years! I was old enough to be his granddaddy almost."

His shipmates were unable to persuade Bob against his intention to stay in Cape Town and not return to Orient with them, so they gave it up as a bad job, and turned their attention to the many young women who were offering more food and drink and promising other favours.

Sailing on to the island of Mauritius

When, other than Bob Styles, all sailors and all passengers had returned to Orient and the wind was fair for her to continue on her journey, Laure and Suzanne and the other cabin passengers stood on the poop deck watching the crew climb the tall masts and inch out along her booms to unfurl the sails. On deck other sailors hauled on ropes and cranked winches to set the foresails and it was not long before the open sea was reached.

In the Indian Ocean Orient was set on course for Madagascar and the island of Mauritius, where she would anchor in Port Louis harbour for a short while before turning south and into the Roaring Forties. These constantly blowing winds would then send her speedily, if uncomfortably for her passengers, onwards to Australia.

"It will be stormy and the steerage passengers will suffer yet again," one of the officers told the cabin passengers. "However," he continued, "three-quarters of the voyage will have been completed by then, and the relief and excitement of being nearer to a better life will outweigh their discomfort to some extent. At least this is what has often been told us by those emigrating. Storms do not take them completely by surprise and they have become accustomed to shipboard life and its vicissitudes."

Now that it would not be long before Suzanne and Laure reached the end of their journey in Douglas' ship, Laure began to feel sad. She knew the parting was inevitable and that she must resign herself to it. She did not want Douglas' last glimpse of her for several months to be one of an unhappy tear stained face. A sailor's wife would need to be very brave as she would frequently need to bid goodbye to her husband when he sailed away on lengthy voyages to China and India as well as to the antipodean colonies.

"I will show him that, although I am young, I can be courageous and patient," Laure told herself. That evening however Douglas found her sitting alone in the saloon and she was looking so forlorn that he went quickly to her side and put his arms around her seeking an explanation for her unhappiness.

"Of course I too shall feel bereft without your presence," he told her on hearing the reason for her dejection, "but just as I will be able, by being occupied in my task as master of Orient, to prevent myself from spending too much time lamenting, so must you, my darling, find work to do which will pass the time enjoyably. What about your piano playing? Will it not be pleasurable to have your piano set up again for you to play the music you love?"

"After so many months away from it I shall need to practise my exercises and scales first so that I regain speed and fluency," said Laure. "That would certainly take my mind away from sad ruminating; but what hard labour it will be!"

"Worthwhile though," said Douglas, "for then you will be back to your previous competence, and able to play all the compositions you wish to. Might you also be able to compose music? Did your studies enable you to do this?"

"Unfortunately not," Laure replied. "It was not thought proper for women to learn such subjects as theory and harmony of music at the Conservatoire. Women were not to become composers. They could only become performers and teachers! Only men were allowed to learn composition and of course conducting."

"How absurd!" Douglas exclaimed.

"Yes indeed," said Laure, "and my aunt Julie Volpéliére, the portraitist who is unmarried, thought that the practice was quite infamous. I believe she wrote to the director of the Conservatoire, but I do not think she received a reply. I have to say that I shared my aunt's opinion, but I was not able to obtain the tuition I wanted, although I angered my tutors by requesting it several times. Do you not think, Douglas, that women ought to have the same opportunities for advancement as men?

When we marry will you allow me to be a person in my own right? Will you listen to my opinions and treat me as your equal?"

Douglas listened in admiration to this quite long speech of Laure's which was spoken entirely in English.

"My dearest Laure," he replied, "when I remember that only three months ago, when we first met each other, you knew only a few words of English, and, having studied diligently since then, you now express yourself with such ease, my only sentiment is one of admiration. I shall never consider myself superior to you in intellect or character. That I am stronger in body than you, I have to admit as my bones and muscles are created thus, so that I can protect you if need be, but you and I shall be equal partners in every other respect in our marriage. We will always discuss matters and only make decisions that we both agree to."

"I am so glad you feel as I do," Laure said. "My father treated my mother as though she was a child. He always did exactly what he wanted to do and was fond of telling her not to trouble her little head about such and such, just to let him in his wisdom decide the best course of action! It used to amuse me a little, but I decided that I would not be able to tolerate being swept aside like that when I married as if I was of no consequence."

Douglas reassured her that in their marriage this would not be the case, and Laure and he embraced before he left her to go to meet his officers and plan Orient's future course towards Mauritius.

Steerage passengers' ablutions

In the steerage quarters Jane Harris was hard at work sewing her husband's new jacket. Once she was sure that the material sat well at the shoulders, she began to insert the right sleeve.

The whole family had enjoyed saltwater baths that morning on deck. George's had consisted of simply being hosed down, but Jane and Georgy had been granted the privacy of a sacking curtain across a corner of the deck and a pail of water. Georgy had been stripped completely, and Jane had had quite a task trying to prevent him from slipping from her grasp and running out onto the deck. She had been ingenuous in using her skirt and blouse to cover herself while still washing herself as thoroughly as she could. The whole manoeuvre was one of the utmost difficulty, and Georgy had received robust scolding from his mother for his disobedient wish to escape. Chastened, he sat at her feet waiting for her to tidy her clothing. They both then made their way to a sunny spot on deck where they sat for a while.

George Harris had gone quickly to his work at the bilge pumps after his hosing, his trousers still wet as it would not have done for the adult males to remove their clothing since women were coming and going to their wash places

OCEAN ADVENTURE 1840

Henry Manning and John Browning's discussion

There was a pleasantly strong wind behind the ship as she turned into the Indian Ocean en route for the southern tip of the island of Madagascar. Douglas from the quarterdeck looked up towards the poop deck where Laure and others were enjoying the fresh breeze and the sunshine. Henry Manning and John Browning were walking up and down, deep in conversation.

"What is the situation regarding education of the young in Australia?" Henry Manning asked. He continued: "I know that the first settlers from England were of the criminal class. Would there have been any education for them?"

"In the late eighteenth and the beginning of this century it was decided that England would rid herself of the entire criminal class by transporting all the convicts to a far off colony. This would then serve as a gaol of no return," John Browning said.

"And amongst the first shipload would have been the children of these convicted criminals no doubt?" Henry asked.

"Yes indeed," replied John, "and it was the fifty children from the first batch of 1500 convicts arriving in Australia about whom a clergyman, Richard Johnson, was so concerned. Although the children were free, they lived under convict conditions with their parents and were treated as members of the criminal class by the ruling elite. The Reverend Johnson started the first school in

1789 and by 1793 there were three more schools under his guidance. It was considered desirable to remove these children from the harmful influence of their parents, and so children as young as three attended these schools where they were taught to read so that they could receive moral instruction from the Bible."

"Those in authority there disapproved of the convict population, then?" asked Henry. "Yes they did, very much so, and in 1802 Governor King established an orphan institution for young girls between the ages of eight and twelve where they were to be discouraged from prostitution by being trained in the values of work, decency, cleanliness and modesty. It was also thought that schooling could be used to foster political loyalty to an established authority, which was an important objective when so many of the inhabitants of the colony were from the criminal classes."

"Children were not able to learn such things from their mothers?" Henry asked.

"The women in the penal colony were treated very badly," John told him. "Even if they had not been prostitutes before landing in Australia, it was thought necessary to transport them to provide for the sexual needs of men who might have left wives behind in England. Therefore they were labelled prostitutes simply because they co-habited with a man without being married to him. A certain Reverend Marsden in 1806 drew up a female register for the colony in which he classified women as either 'married' or 'concubines'. The only marriages he recognised were made in his own church. It was decided by the English government in Australia to fund a school system which was to be run in agreement with the Church of England."

"And the school where you have a position, what type of establishment is it?"

"It is funded by the government in affiliation with the Church of England," John said. "The pupils I shall teach are those of a generation whose grandparents were convicts sent out from England."

"Are any of the pupils children of the rich?" asked Henry.

"No, the wealthy employ tutors and governesses for their children. The children I shall oversee will be taught to keep to the station in life in which they were born."

"So, no possibility for them of advancement?"

"Not as things are now in the colony," John replied.

The two young men continued their discussion. Henry Manning told John Browning what he knew of the position he was going to in Mauritius and what he had learned about the island and its people. "There are Indian, French and Chinese communities there, as well as British," he said. A variety of religions, therefore."

"Slavery was rife until fairly recently, was it not?" John enquired.

"Yes, the abolition of slavery did not occur officially in Mauritius until 1835, although previous to that it had been considered to be illegal. The French plantation owners were using slaves and were very much against giving them their freedom and losing them."

"What happened to the freed slaves in Mauritius?" John asked.

"They were kept working as before, but as apprentices for six years with the same plantation owners, who had to pay them."

Henry went on to explain that the majority of slave-owners were the French who had settled in Mauritius, and John wondered whether Laure's family there would have owned slaves in the past. He felt sure that if she knew how badly these poor people had fared it would make her unhappy. She had, after all, spent all her life in France. John hoped she would not be too discomfited if she found that her Mauritian relations had used slave labour on their properties. By now it was obvious to all the cabin passengers, and quite a few of the steerage passengers, that the young Frenchwoman had a kind heart.

In fact Laure had not been told anything much about life in Mauritius, other than that it was a tropical island subject to typhoons that were terrifying, and that there were mountains where those who could afford it went into the foothills during the hot weather to escape the intense heat and pollution of the towns. She had been told about the giant tortoises found there, and the poor

Dodo bird which had trustingly approached the Dutch settlers in the seventeenth century, and being unable to fly had been captured and eaten into extinction. Of sugar plantations and past slave labour, nothing had been said, only that sugar was one of the main exports of the island. Indentured Indian workers were now brought to Mauritius, contracted to work for a certain number of years before they could return to India, and allowed to bring their wives and families with them. Many remained and settled on the island.

Last lap of the voyage

However much Laure would have liked Orient to slow down her progress, lengthening the hours left with Douglas Wales on his ship, such was not to be. Time passed in its usual inexorable manner. Early one morning she and her mother were packing their cases in readiness to disembark at Port Louis, Mauritius, the next day. The journey from London had taken two and a half months. It was now October and very warm.

"We will need to pack away all our warm clothes," Suzanne said. "It will be too hot in Mauritius to need them. Try to cheer up, *chérie*, if only for my sake. I know you do not wish to be parted from your fiancé so soon, but I am quite sad too at having left France and my way of life there. I do not look forward to having to accept my sister's offer of board and lodging because I cannot support us both now."

"It won't be long, *Maman*," said Laure, "before Douglas will come and rescue us from Tante Marie. Think how pleasurable you will find it to tell her and the other relations that you are going to have such a son-in-law as Douglas who will find us a house and perhaps even one or two servants to help us in it."

Suzanne smiled a little and then said, "I have written a letter to your father that I shall send as soon as we arrive on the island. I have told him that Captain Wales is an honourable man who commands respect from all who know him. I have added also that it would make both you and me very happy if we could have his blessing on your betrothal and that we hope he will at least visit you one day and see for himself how happy you are to be loved by such a man."

"Oh *Maman*, that was so good of you!" said Laure. "Surely he cannot turn away from me forever. One must be prepared though for this to happen, but I shall not give up hope of reconciliation in the future. I know how hard it must have been for you to write to him thus. He has wronged you so dreadfully. Thank you, my dear *Maman*, for putting aside your own feelings so that you can help me to be happy."

That evening the cabin passengers gathered around Suzanne and Laure to bid them farewell. The Walters and the Sedgwicks were only able to give post-restante addresses in Melbourne. "We will send proper addresses once we have them," said Agnes to Laure. Laure gave her aunt's address in Cassis, Mauritius, to the young couples, and also, to his surprise and pleasure, to John Browning.

"I shall always be grateful to you, John," she said, "for your help with the English language, the interesting books you have suggested I should read and your patience with my grammatical errors. Both Douglas and I would be interested to hear about your life in Australia when you are settled in."

The young man promised to write to them both, however bittersweet such contact would be. He was thankful however that friendship was possible, even if romantic love had been out of his reach.

Laure was glad that Henry Manning would also be ending his journey in Mauritius. She felt that his presence there would represent a link with Douglas and the journey on Orient. They would have much to reminisce about, and since she was now contemplating leaving the Catholic Church for the Church of England she would benefit from talks with Henry on religious matters. Henry's curacy was at the Anglican church in Poudriére Street, built on the site of an old French powder magazine and given to the Anglican community by the first governor, Sir Robert Farquhar, for the erection of a church. This church opened for the first time for divine service on Christmas Day 1831. Laure intended to make a point of attending the services there.

Arriving in Port Louis harbour

The three passengers who were to disembark at Port Louis harbour were ready on deck the next morning. Orient's anchor was dropped some two ship's lengths off the quay.

One of the port captain's boats took the stern lines ashore and made them fast on the jetty, and then Orient's stern was hauled close enough to enable gangways to be used. There were a good number of sailing ships at anchor already, and small craft dodged about them, bringing goods to ships and crew members to shore. Passengers alighted down the gangways onto the quay where many donkeys were harnessed to carts, and their Indian and African drivers waited for employment of whatever kind came their way. Douglas had arranged to have the Volpélière ladies' luggage and Laure's portrait brought up to the main deck from the hold of the ship, and he saw it delivered safely into one of the donkey carts and sent on its way to her aunt's house in Cassis, with the necessary payment promised on delivery. Her Pleyel grand piano would follow on a bullock cart.

Suzanne's sister, Marie Bavot, née Bérichon, was on the quayside waiting for her relations in a small four wheeled carriage with a fine looking bay horse harnessed to it. The hood of the carriage was down and Marie was holding a lilac coloured parasol open above her head to protect her from the strong sunshine that was beating down. The driver of the carriage stood beside his horse, with a groom at the ready to assist the passengers.

"My dearest Douglas," said Laure bravely, looking up into his face, "now we must say *au revoir* and I must wish you a safe onward journey to Australia."

Douglas took her in his arms and kissed her tenderly. "I shall count the days until I can return to Mauritius and hold you close again," he said. "Go, my dearest, join your aunt, and remember that I love you and that soon we will be reunited." Laure moved away from him reluctantly, and looking back once or twice she walked to the carriage where Suzanne had already taken her place next to her sister.

Douglas stood and watched as the carriage left in the direction of the town on its way to the home of Madame Bavot. The three open parasols prevented him from seeing the ladies' faces clearly, but he saw that Laure had turned back to wave a handkerchief, so he bowed hand on heart. Only once the carriage was out of sight did he stride off to the custom house where he had a meeting arranged.

Laure waits

The weeks Laure spent in her aunt's house in Cassis while she waited for Douglas' return were a pleasant change from being on the ship and compensated for the separation from him. Charles Bavot, her uncle by marriage, owned a share in a sugar plantation nearby, where until 1835 his slaves worked in the fields and in the house. Now the three women who worked in the house were emancipated and were paid for their labour. They had been with the family for many years and, having been treated well, were happy to continue with their duties as before, as were the four male former slaves who did the gardening, saw to the horses and helped with the heavy work both in and out of the house. The Bavots had treated their African slaves well, providing decent living conditions, schooling for their children and medical treatment on their estate.

Suzanne especially enjoyed the attentions of the young woman, Joséphine, who did her laundry, looked after her clothes and brought coffee to her room in the morning. Laure's piano had been reassembled and placed in a room whose French window opened onto a large garden, and she enjoyed walking in the garden when she had finished her piano practice. Laure was keeping a diary in which she wrote every day of her activities and also of her feelings about Douglas, his return and their marriage. She would share it with him when she next saw him.

Monsieur and Madame Bavot, at first dismayed that Laure was engaged to an older man who was a foreigner and of a different religion, expressed their concern initially to Suzanne. Gradually, as had happened in Suzanne's case earlier, they realized that there were more advantages than disadvantages to the match. Marie Bavot then generously stepped in and offered to pay for a trousseau and the wedding dress. Her husband, who saw the benefit he would gain in having a family member with a trading ship, agreed entirely. One of the house servants, Francoise, was good with the needle so the fashioning of nightgowns, petticoats and other undergarments was started almost immediately. Laure was persuaded to learn how neatly to attach lace trimmings and sew a seam, which helped to pass the time. Fashion magazines were pored over for the future wedding dress.

One day a letter came from Henri Volpélière in reply to Suzanne's. He expressed concern and wrote that he did not feel able to give his consent to an early marriage without having met this Captain Douglas Wales. Laure was despondent. Suzanne said it was only to be expected, but that at least the subject had been broached. Henri, she said, had not written in anger nor had he insisted that the engagement be broken. He was sitting on the fence. Continued patience was needed.

Douglas takes Peter, James and George ashore at Melbourne

Several weeks later, the day after Orient arrived at Port Phillip, Melbourne Douglas went ashore, taking in the boat Peter Sedgwick, James Walters, George Harris and some of his officers. He had decided which of the businessmen of his acquaintance should be asked to interview Peter Sedgwick and George Harris and perhaps assist them in their quest for employment.

Although George Harris' previous experience would render him more suitable for agricultural work and animal husbandry, Douglas went with him to meet a businessman who kept a shop in Port Phillip. Because Jane Harris would be working in Melbourne (to help with the birth of the Walters' child) and as cattle farms were situated on the outskirts of that town, George would have had to reside away from his wife if he were to obtain work of that sort which would not have been good for the family.

Leaving George waiting to be interviewed, Douglas then took Peter to meet a gentleman who was buying and selling land. His business was thriving and he needed another accountant. Having observed them on the long voyage in Orient, Douglas' recommendation was sufficient reference for both Peter and George, and both were offered employment.

James Walters was accepted at once by the merchant to whom he had a letter of introduction from his employer in England. James was very pleased to be assured by him that there were good and reasonably priced lodgings nearby where he and Agnes could stay until they were able to afford better accommodation. The three young men returned later to the ship in a very cheerful mood which was echoed by their wives on hearing the good news. James had also been given the name of a doctor in Melbourne by Surgeon Superintendent Grant, a welcome recommendation for Agnes' care, if needed, at the birth of her child.

"Do you think your new jacket helped in your getting taken on?" Jane Harris asked her husband. He replied, "Well, it helped me to feel smarter looking, and so I expect I made a good fist at presenting myself for what will be a very different sort of work for me, in a shop."

"What will your duties be?" asked Jane.

"The shopkeeper told me that he needs a strong fellow to carry sacks of grain and potatoes and suchlike. He also said that he could do with an extra hand behind the counter because he is becoming too busy to manage on his own. But best of all, when I told him that I was married, with a young son too, he said there's two small rooms in the top floor of the building that we can have, and that in return for some extra tasks about the house as well as the shop we will not have to pay much in the way of rent."

"That is very good indeed," said Jane; "it is far more than we could have expected at the start of our journey."

Agnes and Anne were extremely relieved that their husbands had found work ever so quickly, and Agnes was delighted to hear that they would not have to take their chances in a tent after all, and that Jane would be living nearby and able to help her with the birth of her child.

First Reunion of Douglas and Laure

Soon after Orient docked in Port Louis harbour on her return from Melbourne, Douglas hired a horse and rode to Cassis. He was received rapturously by Laure who proudly introduced him to Charles and Marie Bavot. The French couple were impressed with the tall handsome Englishman and found his manners impeccable. Douglas, in what free time he had for himself in the intervening weeks, had tried his best to brush up his French. He had succeeded grammatically and improved his vocabulary, but his accent was not of the best. "Never mind, my dear," Marie said to Charles when they were alone again. "When they are married, Laure will be able to help him with French pronunciation." Her husband did not think the matter important at all. He took Douglas at face value, found him interesting and knowledgeable and enjoyed discussing trade matters with him.

"I think I shall write to Henri Volpélière and convey to him my opinion of his daughter's English fiancé," he told his wife. "I am impressed with Captain Wales' honourable bearing and his courtesy. It is clear that he has behaved with the utmost propriety towards Laure throughout the long journey, where a lesser man might have given in to the numerous temptations there must surely have been during it. Suzanne has told me that at no time did the captain try to take advantage of Laure's obvious affection for him."

"He is also prepared to take my sister into his home when he marries Laure," said Marie. "That will make life so much easier for her. It would have been awkward for Suzanne to have had no alternative but to depend on us in every way."

The wedding

Eventually, but much too slowly for Laure, time passed. Douglas sailed away and returned to Mauritius several times during the three years until her twenty-first birthday. On his last return Laure, Suzanne and all in the Bavot household were in a state of high excitement because now the wedding could go ahead.

Laure's father had sent word that he was relieved to hear from Charles Bavot that Captain Wales was a decent fellow, and that he, Henri, fully intended to return to Mauritius one day before too long to visit his daughter.

This he would do, he said, even though the rest of the family, in particular his own father, had decided to turn their backs permanently on Laure. Henri would be unable to be at the wedding however: that would be too contentious. Charles Bavot would give Laure away. Suzanne was heard to say that Henri had thus been able to wriggle out of any responsibility for giving or withholding permission for the marriage, in a way that was totally in keeping with his character. "I've no doubt that he will impress upon his father that a visit to Mauritius, after the marriage has taken place, is necessary for reasons other than seeing his only child. Financial reasons, perhaps, or any other reasons he can think up. He can visit with impunity once the marriage is a *fait-a-complis!*" Sadly Laure had to agree that this was a correct summing up of her father's motivations, but she was happy that she would see him again one day.

Laure and Douglas, in the weeks before the wedding, which was to take place on 12th July 1843, went looking for a house to rent that would be their first home. As Laure sat beside Douglas, with reins in hand, in the Bavot's open carriage, she thought she must be the happiest young woman in Mauritius; and when they found a house they liked, in the foothills of the Moka range of mountains, she threw her arms around him and covered his face with kisses, which Douglas, laughing, returned. Completely happy they returned to her aunt, uncle and mother where they all sat down to dinner and a discussion of what would be needed for the house took place. Douglas announced that he would cover the cost of everything in the way of furniture and fittings and would engage servants for it.

Now all that was needed was to go through the contract of marriage, and then the wedding. At that time it was a requirement of French law that, if a Frenchwoman married a foreigner, they must go before a notary, (in Douglas and Laure's case a Monsieur Jollivet), and have drawn up a legal document stating what each brought to the marriage in the way of worldly goods. The document was witnessed by ten people, including Laure's aunt and mother, and two of Douglas' friends, Guy Robinson and William Cook.

The wedding took place, as Douglas had said it would in the Anglican Church in Poudriére Street, and there were many people in the congregation. Henry Manning was amongst them. Laure looked delightful in her wedding dress of simple white muslin copied by a dressmaker from one of the fashionable drawings sent from Paris. True to her word Marie Bavot had made sure that her niece lacked for nothing in the way of a trousseau and a wedding dress. The reception took place in the Bavot's house.

Very soon after the wedding Douglas was due to sail Orient on another voyage, so Laure, at last, would be able to journey with him.

They spent the night after their wedding in a hotel in Port Louis. After dining in style they exchanged loving glances with each other, talking softly about the wedding and the guests who had been there. Douglas said, "I wish my mother had been present. I know she would have been enchanted with you. You looked so beautiful in your wedding dress, and particularly so when you were unveiled and walking beside me down the aisle. I was so proud to be at your side."

"I too should have liked to have had your mother's attendance at our wedding," Laure said, "then she could have shared my pride and happiness at having such a handsome husband, and she, such a son. As soon as we can, we should have daguerreotype images made of ourselves as we are now to show those who were too far away to attend our happy day."

"I am sorry that we cannot have a longer honeymoon here," Douglas said. "But, my darling, I couldn't be happier that we shall be together in Orient," replied Laure. "To be husband and wife in the vessel in which we first made each other's acquaintance. Surely no honeymoon could be more romantic! Think of seeing the moon racing across the sky as we surge forward at night towards the horizon, or rising from our bed at sunrise to glory in its rays and then watching the fiery globe descend at sunset surrounded by pink tinged clouds."

"I am glad you feel as you do," said Douglas. "It seems that you are cut out to be a master mariner's wife. I am a lucky man."

Their love for each other soon overcame any shyness or nervousness that the young Laure experienced when they went up to the hotel bedroom after dinner. In the morning Laure, in her husband's arms, felt glad that she was now wife of a good kind man, and she thanked her Maker that their paths had crossed and that their life would continue together. They boarded Orient that afternoon where a comfortable suite of rooms had been made ready for them. There was the bedroom with a large and comfortable double bed. It also contained cupboards and a chest of drawers. Off the bedroom was the water closet and washstand. Leading off the bedroom was a small sitting room, and Laure cried out in delight when she saw the upright piano situated in its corner. She approved of the comfortable armchairs and small dining table.

"This will make a very good first home for us," she told Douglas.

Once the ship had set sail, Douglas' energies were given over to his command of Orient. Laure sometimes took her place at Douglas' side on the quarterdeck, watching the crew at work. Dinner was shared occasionally with the cabin passengers, but more frequently they dined alone, spending any free evenings reading and writing in the comfortable salon near the Great Cabin.

Laure's interest in Homeopathy

Dr Grant was the surgeon superintendent on this journey too, and he found in Laure an enthusiastic student. She took a great interest in the welfare of the emigrants, the children in particular, and was excited when Dr Grant lent her a book written by Samuel Hahnemann, entitled 'Indications of the Homeopathic Employment of Medicines in Ordinary Practice', published in 1807. Dr Hahnemann became dissatisfied with the state of medicine in his time. He claimed that the medicine he had been taught to practise sometimes did the patient more harm than good. He had found that the use of certain plants obtained cures in certain diseases, and he gave this principle the name 'homeopathy'.

In a mild and safe way Dr Grant tried out some of the homeopathic principles on sick passengers of all ages, and found that his patients' symptoms really did improve. He and Laure had many interesting discussions, and Laure was pleased when she realized that her husband's instructions, regarding the health of his passengers and his crew, followed Dr Hahnemann's recommendations that patients' should receive a proper diet, bed rest, fresh air and sunshine, and good hygiene.

Mary Suzanne

It was not long into her marriage to Douglas that Laure found she was expecting their first child. They were both delighted. Their daughter, Mary Suzanne, was born on board when Orient was anchored in the Bay of Bengal.

"We still have months of journeying," Douglas said. "I would not be surprised if this little girl will take her first steps on the decks of our ship. She will adapt to the moving deck, so much so indeed that when we reach land she, being unused to a static surface, may well lose her balance and fall more frequently."

"You or I will then pick her up and kiss her," his wife replied.

They stood on deck, Mary in Laure's arms, and Douglas' arm around Laure. All around them the crew worked the sails, some of the assisted emigrants took their turn at being out in the fresh air, animals were fed and watered; a cow was milked. The captain took pleasure in knowing that he always had done, and always would do, his very best for his beloved family and for all the passengers and crew on his ship. As he looked down on the downy head of his daughter, she moved her head and looked up at him. Her blue eyes looked directly into his, and she smiled at him for the first time.

BIBLIOGRAPHY & REFERENCES

The late Professor James McConville
Advice on shipboard life in the 19th Century

Patrick Wales-Smith
Advice on nautical matters

Father Andrew Foster
Religious advice

Professor Clive Wilkinson
Climatic Research Unit University of East Anglia
Seasonal Routes taken from UK to India & China & ships bound for Australia, & advice regarding "sailing directions"

Jonathan Binns Were CMG
A Voyage from Plymouth to Melbourne in 1839

Thomas Wilsmore's Diary
Journey from England to Melbourne 1841
Library of Western Australia (Containing a copy of Captain Douglas Wales' own account of a Mutiny on board "Orient")

Donal Baird
Women at Sea in the Age of Sail

The British Library
The Somerset Years
Florence Chuk

Dr Margaret Makepeace: information about the sailings and arrivals of the ship "Orient" from digitized newspapers of the time

Photocopies of engravings and text from the Illustrated London News

National Maritime Museum
Accommodation in Wooden Sailing Ships illustrated with plates of shipboard scenes.

Lloyd's Register of Shipping & National Archives
Passenger Lists

INTERNET SOURCES

Jansen, Elizabeth
They came by Ship "Orient" as self-funded & and Bounty immigrants in l840
http://www.oocities.org/vic/847/40ori40.ntm

Early Victorian Women's Hats, Bonnets and Dresses
http://www.katetattersall.com
Shutterstock Images 1840s Victorian Dress

OCEAN ADVENTURE 1840

Resource Package supporting SOUTHWARD BOUND display at South Australian Maritime Museum – a simple overall view of migration to South Australia circa 1840

On the Water, Maritime Nation 1800-1950
http://amhistory.Si.edu/onthewater/exhibition/2_3htm

www.castleofgoodhope.co.za/history.htm

Information about shipboard provisions
www.norwayheritage.com/provisions.htm

http:/www.homeed.vic.edu.au/2003/10/30australian-schooling-a-history-of etc

Jigger-Mast, History,
http://en.wikipedia.org/wiki/Bowsprit,

www.blueskyteducation.co.uk

History of Anglican Church in Mauritius
http:/www.swizznetafrica.com/workdone/DioceseofMauritius/index.php

http://wwww.tallshiprose.org/info/tour/virtualtour/greatcabin.html

The Voyage Out: Life on Board an Emigrant Ship
http://freepages.genealogy.rootsweb.ancestry.com/ourstuff

Letter from Schoolmaster on "Mermaid" sailing to New Zealand http://graham-hay.blogspot.co.uk(2012/10/1864-letter-from-schoolmaster-on.html

Life onboard an immigrant ship during the 1800s
http://wwww.samemory.sa.gov.au/site/page.cfm

Coat of the uniform of an East India Company Commander made in l832
http://www.rng.co.uk/server/show/conMediaFile.3230

Wooden walls and iron sides – South Australia's maritime history: Immigrant shipping
http://en.wikipedia.org.wiki/File:

ABOUT THE AUTHOR

Gillian Noakes lives in London. She was born, and spent her early years in Monaco, France starting her education there at the Lycée in Monte Carlo.

She trained as a pianist at the Conservatorio Benedetto Marcello in Venice, Italy and at the Guildhall School of Music and Middlesex University in London. She teaches the piano privately.

She is the great-granddaughter of Douglas and Laure Wales.

Printed in Great Britain
by Amazon.co.uk, Ltd.,
Marston Gate.